# Oak Island
### And The
## *Mayflower*

# Oak Island
## And The
# *Mayflower*

Written and published by
James A. McQuiston, FSA Scot
jamesamcquiston@gmail.com

*We come on a ship they called Mayflower*

*We come on a ship that sailed the moon*

*We come in the ages' most uncertain hours*

*And sing an American tune*

– Paul Simon
*American Tune*

# TABLE OF CONTENTS

# PREFACE

When I first set out to provide a simple but important piece of information to the current Oak Island, Nova Scotia, treasure hunting team back in the fall of 2016, I never intended to write a single book, let alone six on the subject of this 225-year-old treasure hunt.

I also never dreamed I would appear on the History Channel's hit TV show *The Curse of Oak Island*, not just once, but many times.

That single bit of information I provided has blended with four visits to Nova Scotia, three to Scotland, and ten days on Oak Island, with even more days spent at other important locations in Nova Scotia like the New Ross foundation, the Nova Scotia Archives, the College of Geographic Sciences, and at Port Royal, NS, where forts provided shelter to French, Scottish and English settlers at various times in its existence.

I also traveled to the New England states of Maine, Massachusetts, New Hampshire and Connecticut, not realizing at the time that there was such an intimate connection of these states to Nova Scotia's history, and more specifically to the early settlement and treasure hunting that has taken place on Oak Island.

This last realization is the subject of this book.

It is a fact that Nova Scotia, as named, and as first settled by Scottish adventurers, would not likely have existed had it not been for the folks who arrived in America aboard the ship *Mayflower*.

This seems like a pretty bold statement that would require a lot of proof, which I intend to provide.

It is conversely true that many of the earliest landowners and most famous treasure hunters on Oak Island have a direct relationship to the area of Plymouth, Massachusetts, and, in some cases, directly to signers of the **Mayflower Compact**.

The year 2020 celebrates the 400th anniversary of the landing of the Pilgrims at Plymouth Rock. The year 2021 celebrates the 400th anniversary of the establishment of the Canadian province of Nova Scotia.

These two events are intricately tied to each other in a series of amazing and interdependent ways.

In the big picture, it was for the protection of the *Mayflower* passengers, as it concerned one of the main economic supporters and absentee leaders of the Plymouth Colony, that led King James I of England and Ireland (also James VI of Scotland) to grant the land that the French then called Acadia to Sir William Alexander as New Scotland or, in Latin, *Nova Scotia*.

This series of events has been hidden away in many documents and aged books, where perhaps only the most avid historian would find them.

It is my hope to simplify the story so that all people interested in either historic event can understand this important connection.

Even with all of my visits to Nova Scotia and New England, and after the writing of five earlier books on Oak Island, it took nearly four years for the significant connection of these two major historic events (and the subsequent settlement and exploration of Oak Island) to sink into my own curious mind.

It wasn't until my fourth book, *Oak Island Endgame*, that I started appreciating important family connections and, not even realizing it, I began to approach the Oak Island mystery from an entirely new point of view.

I had previously been focused on the background history of a Scottish settlement in Nova Scotia dating to the early 1600s, and how that might have led to a cache of treasure and other items being buried on Oak Island to await a possible recovery at a later time.

I then changed my approach to exploring those families who came to the island to settle and/or seek treasure there, beginning about the mid 1700s, and extending into the 1800s, and beyond.

Along the way, I realized there was also considerable information on what happened at least in Nova Scotia, if not always directly on Oak Island, between these two eras in history.

I once heard Marty Lagina, one of the main forces behind the current Oak Island search, remind his fellow treasure hunters that it is a common trait of theorists to find clues everywhere that support their particular theory. I do not plead innocent to this tendency, but the sheer amount of information I have uncovered seems to outweigh any possible prejudice on my part.

The history is fascinating, it is broad in its coverage of events, and it seems to present an undeniable link between those families who settled at or near Plymouth, Massachusetts, and those who later settled and/or searched for treasure on Oak Island, Nova Scotia, in the years to come.

As a means of establishing my credibility, I was honored with a fellowship by the Society of Antiquaries of Scotland in 2014, based on my many years of writing books and articles that had some Scottish historic link to them. As a fellow, I enjoy access to the National Museum of Scotland and the National Records of Scotland.

Held within these three organizations is a vast collection of Scottish history, and I have been aided by the staff members of these institutions many times.

Having my fellowship also opened doors for me not only with the Oak Island team, but also with the British Museum, the Gustavianum Museum in Sweden, the Nova Scotia Archives, the library of the Nova Scotia College of Geographic Sciences (home to many old maps and books on Scottish/Nova Scotian history), and to individuals like Kel Hancock, the Grand Historian of the Grand Lodges of Freemasonry in Nova Scotia, and many other significant Oak Island historians and authors.

Using historic records, land charters, Privy Council minutes, Freemasonry minutes, private letters, and old books (some dating into the early 1600s), I have pieced together this theory and the facts that support it.

Of course, I hope that the reader will not only enjoy the story but also consider the significance of it all.

*Chapter One*

# GORGES, ALEXANDER AND BACON

Ferdinando Gorges is a name sounding decidedly non English in origin. In fact, Ferdinando was maternally related to the Gorges line, which had come to England from France during the 11th century invasion by William the Conqueror.

When the last living member of the English branch of Gorges was on his death bed, with no children to follow him, he turned to the son of his sister, one Theobald Russell, and offered Russell all of his estates if he would adopt the Gorges name instead of Russell.

Theobald did this, and from his direct line came Ferdinando Gorges in 1565, son of Edward Gorges by his wife Cicely Lygon.

The brother of Cicely was named Ferdinando Lygon and both of these names, Ferdinando and Lygon, had come to England by way of Spain. Ferdinando Gorges immortalized the Lygon side of his family by establishing a short-lived colony named Lygonia in what is now Maine, directly across the water from Nova Scotia.

Ferdinando Gorges, the man with the "foreign" sounding name, was extremely instrumental in the settling of both New England and New Scotland (Nova Scotia) with English speaking immigrants.

Gorges was a military commander, and governor of a port city also named Plymouth, located in England.

His early involvement in English trade and the settlement of North America, as well as his efforts in establishing the Plymouth Colony in New England, in founding the Province of Maine, and in encouraging the settlement of Nova Scotia by Scotsmen, earned him the title of "Father of English Colonization in North America," even though Gorges himself never set foot in the New World.

After a long military career, especially in fields of battle throughout Europe, Gorges was rewarded for his services with a knighthood, and with the post of governor of the fort at Plymouth, England, a position he held for many years.

During the Spanish Armada attack, Gorges was able to raise the alarm that enabled the defense of the country, although autumn storms helped make sure that the Spanish fleet was sufficiently damaged. Ferdinando's alertness gained him additional fame and attention.

Gorges's interest in colonization began when Captain George Weymouth, an early explorer of the New England coastline, brought to England three captured Native Americans, one by the name of Epenow.

Gorges was given Epenow as his slave.

He described Epenow as "a person of goodly stature, strong and well-proportioned," as well as brave, stout and sober. Epenow was also clever. Gorges took Epenow as his own slave and housed him with another Native, Assacumet, who taught Epenow the English language.

Epenow tricked Gorges into thinking that he could lead his master to a gold mine on Martha's Vineyard.

Perhaps surprising to some, *Mayflower* immigrants were not the first to attempt a settlement in New England. Explorer Bartholomew Gosnold founded a very short-lived community at a place called Cuttyhunk Island in 1602. He is the very man who discovered and named Cape Cod, Martha's Vineyard (after his deceased daughter Martha), and the Elizabeth Islands.

After only a few months of hardship and exploration, Gosnold's group returned to England. He later became a top leader in the Jamestown Colony of Virginia.

An interesting connection is that Gosnold was the son of Anthony Gosnold and Dorothy Bacon.

Henry Gosnold, a famous friend of Sir Francis Bacon, was Bartholomew's cousin. The village of Hessett, where Dorothy was born, is in the same county of Suffolk as Barham, England, where Sir Francis Bacon's father lived; and so there is a high likelihood that Dorothy was some type of cousin to Sir Francis Bacon as well – same county, same surname, same friends and family. Dorothy even had an uncle also named Francis Bacon.

We will see how Sir Francis Bacon fits into the Plymouth scheme very shortly.

In 1606, King James granted the Elizabeth Islands to the Council of New England, on which Sir William Alexander, founder of Nova Scotia, served.

This council was finally dissolved in 1635. After this, Cuttyhunk and the Elizabeth Islands became the sole property of Sir William Alexander.

As of 1635, Alexander was also owner of Long Island, New York, including most of what is now New York City, and later claimed Long Island, Massachusetts.

As for Epenow, Gorges took his bait of a gold mine in the New World. He commissioned a voyage to Martha's Vineyard with Epenow and a few other Natives going along as translators and guides. Also backing the trip were one of William Shakespeare's sponsors, the Earl of Southampton, and also Captain Nicholas Hobson.

According to the New England Historical Society, Gorges didn't completely trust his Native slave. He ordered Hobson to guard him closely and to dress him in long clothing so Epenow could be grabbed easily.

When Hobson sailed into the harbor at Martha's Vineyard, Epenow's people greeted the vessel peacefully. Hobson invited them aboard ship.

Once his friends came on deck, Epenow quietly hatched an escape plan with them. The Natives told Hobson they'd soon return with trade goods.

The next day, they arrived in 20 canoes, but refused to board the ship. Hobson talked and gestured, but they remained standoffish. Hobson called Epenow out of the hold of the ship to translate.

Epenow welcomed his people in English, which they didn't understand, and instructed them in his own tongue, which the English didn't understand. Then he tried to lunge off the ship. The crew grabbed hold of his clothing, but he was so big and heavy he went overboard. When he hit water, the Natives shot arrows at the ship. The English returned fire, killing some of the attackers.

Captain Hobson and the crew were wounded and the ship returned to England without any gold or Native slaves. Hobson told Gorges that Epenow was dead.

"Thus were my hopes of that particular (situation) made void and frustrate," wrote Gorges.

Alive and well, Epenow had no use for the English and, from then on, he led the Native resistance to them.

In 1619, the year before the *Mayflower* arrived, Captain Thomas Dermer came to Martha's Vineyard. Epenow visited with him peacefully and told him, laughingly, about his escape.

Dermer returned the next year, shortly before the Pilgrims arrived. Another Native captive named Squanto was aboard his ship.

Epenow's men, not so friendly this time, attacked Dermer and his crew. They rescued Squanto and killed all but one of Dermer's men. Dermer himself was wounded and escaped to Virginia, where he died.

Gorges later obtained a patent for a huge tract of land (Lygonia) which eventually became part of Maine.

He never set foot in the New World, but he seemed to understand that capturing and enslaving Native Americans had consequences. Gorges wrote of – "A war now new begun between the inhabitants of those parts, and us."

In 1607, as a shareholder in the Plymouth Company, Gorges helped fund the failed Popham Colony, located near present-day Phippsburg, Maine, which was named for William Phips, another man often linked with Oak Island.

The Plymouth Company was an English stock company founded in 1606 by James I. It consisted of knights, merchants, adventurers and planters from the cities of Bristol, Exeter and Plymouth.

Its purpose was to establish settlements on the coast of North America, between 38 and 45 degrees north latitude, within 100 miles of the seaboard. The merchants agreed to finance the settlers' trip in return for repayment of their expenses plus interest out of the profits made.

In 1620, after years of disuse, the company was revived and reorganized as the Plymouth Council for New England with a new charter – the New England Charter of 1620. The Plymouth Company had forty patentees at that point, and established the Council for New England to oversee their efforts. One of these patentees was Sir William Alexander.

On July 23, 1620, several months before the *Mayflower* landed at Plymouth, New England, Ferdinando Gorges was able to get a directive written and signed by some very illustrious people. The directive read:

> *Whereas it is thought fit that a Patent of Incorporation be granted to the adventurers of the Northern Colony in Virginia, to contain the like liberties, privileges, power, authorities, lands and all other things within their limits, namely, between the degrees of forty and forty-eight… this new Company is to be free of custom and subsidy for the like term of years, and of impositions after so long a time as his Majesty shall please to grant unto them. Dated 23d July, 1620*

This "new Company" became the Plymouth Colony, named after Gorges's home port of Plymouth, England.

The signatures were general in nature and included nine men who signed this way:

| | |
|---|---|
| *Lord Chancellor* | *Lord Digby* |
| *Lord Privy Seal* | *Mr. Comptroller* |
| *Earl of Arundell* | *Mr. Secretary Naunton* |
| *Mr. Secretary Calvert* | *Master of the Wards* |
| *Master of the Rolls* | |

And guess who the Lord Chancellor was in 1620 - Sir Francis Bacon, the very first man to sign this request to create the Plymouth Colony.

Back on May 23, 1609, Sir Francis Bacon had drafted a new charter for the Virginia Colony, and now he was leading the charge to create the Plymouth Colony.

As Lord Chancellor, Bacon was essentially the next most powerful man to King James when he signed this 1620 directive that began the process of establishing the Plymouth Colony.

Bacon served as Lord Chancellor from March 7, 1617, until 1621, when he was brought up on possibly false charges and imprisoned by his enemies.

One of the investors and councilmen of the Plymouth Colony was William Alexander, who, at the time, was also highly placed in the court of King James.

Based on *The Freemasons Repository*, the *Documentary History of the State of Maine, Cracroft's Peerage,* and *The Peerage of Scotland*, William Alexander was a member of the Great Council of Plymouth.

Bacon and Alexander were also both serving on the Privy Council of King James at the time, and I've drawn many parallels in the lives of these two men, but the current subject shows another very close connection.

And so, in this one document from the summer of 1620, you have the three subjects of this chapter all involved, in a most serious way, with the settlement of America, particularly at Plymouth, in New England.

The third signature on the document, that of the Earl of Arundel, was written by Sir Thomas Howard, 2nd Earl of Arundel.

Howard was also on the New England Plantations Committee in 1620. The following year he presided over the House of Lords Committee, in April 1621, for investigating the charges against Sir Francis Bacon and, at whose demise, he was appointed a commissioner of the great seal – essentially a committee to handle some of the Lord Chancellor's duties until a new one could be appointed to replace Bacon.

Sir Francis Bacon was notably responsible for creating the Plymouth Colony, and it was the Plymouth Colony, invested in and counselled by Sir William Alexander, that urged the king to give Nova Scotia to Alexander the following year, particularly through the encouragement of its leader Sir Ferdinando Gorges.

The stage was now set for the arrival of the *Mayflower* and its mainly Puritan occupants. Their desire to travel to America was seen as audacious and risky, as previous attempts to settle in North America, both in the Plymouth Colony and the Virginia Colony, had failed.

Originally, there was only one colony named Virginia for the "Virgin Queen " – Queen Elizabeth. This colony was then split into two regions, north and south. The dividing line was basically the 40th degree of latitude, although this dividing point was often in contention, and the original Plymouth Colony mandate stated between 38 and 45 degrees north latitude.

Jamestown, founded in 1607 and located well below 40 degrees, saw most of its settlers perish within the first year, with 440 of the 500 new arrivals dying of starvation during the first six months of winter.

The Puritans above the 40th parallel would also learn of starvation, as well as the constant threat of attacks by indigenous people. But despite all of the arguments against traveling to this new land, their conviction that God wanted them to go held sway. They wrote –

*We verily believe and trust the Lord is with us, and that He will graciously prosper our endeavors according to the simplicity of our hearts therein.*

The *Mayflower* was the English ship that transported the first Puritans (known today as the Pilgrims) from England to the New World in 1620. After a grueling ten weeks at sea, the *Mayflower*, with 102 passengers and a crew of about 30, reached America, dropping anchor near the tip of Cape Cod, on November 11, 1620.

The *Speedwell*, the sister ship to the *Mayflower* (later purchased and captained by John Chappell), had to turn back to England because of a leak, leaving the *Mayflower* to make the treacherous journey on her own.

Fans of the Oak Island mystery will recognize the name Chappell in the form of the brothers William and Renwick Chappell, and William's son, Mel Chappell, who were some of the most famous treasure hunters on Oak Island. They were descendants of the new purchaser of the damaged *Speedwell*, as will soon be explained.

The Pilgrims had originally hoped to reach America in early October using two ships, but the *Speedwell's* problems meant they could sail only on the *Mayflower*.

Eleven passengers from the *Speedwell* boarded the *Mayflower*. Arriving November 11th, the immigrants were forced to survive somewhat unprepared through a harsh winter. As a result, only half of the original Pilgrims made it through the first winter at Plymouth.

At first, a small group landed ashore in various places to decide on the best location to bring the ship closer to shore, and to make a permanent settlement. They used a smaller sailing vessel and, on their third trip, took temporary shelter near a place where they had seen Native Americans cleaning an orca or dolphin that had washed ashore. Aboard the vessel were at least two ancestors of future president Franklin Delano Roosevelt – Thomas Howland and Richard Warren.

In the morning the men were attacked with a hail of arrows. They fired back with their guns but, luckily for both sides, no one was killed. It is recorded that they kept some of these arrows to ship back to their families in England as mementos. They noted that the tips of some arrows were of brass, but others were of deer antler tips, and others were of eagle claws.

The Pilgrims created and signed the **Mayflower Compact** while still on the *Mayflower*. This compact was an agreement made among the passengers before going ashore to establish a rudimentary form of democracy in which each member would contribute to the safety and welfare of the planned settlement.

The full text of the **Mayflower Compact** reads:

*In the name of God, Amen. We, whose names are underwritten, the Loyal Subjects of our dread Sovereign Lord King James, by the Grace of God, of Great Britain, France, and Ireland, King, defender of the Faith, etc.:*

*Having undertaken, for the Glory of God, and advancements of the Christian faith, and the honor of our King and Country, a voyage to plant the first colony in the Northern parts of Virginia; do by these presents, solemnly and mutually, in the presence of God, and one another; covenant and combine ourselves together into a civil body politic; for our better ordering, and preservation and furtherance of the ends aforesaid; and by virtue hereof to enact, constitute, and frame, such just and equal laws, ordinances, acts, constitutions, and offices, from time to time, as shall be thought most meet and convenient for the general good of the colony; unto which we promise all due submission and obedience.*

*In witness whereof we have hereunto subscribed our names at Cape Cod the 11th of November, in the year of the reign of our Sovereign Lord King James, of England, France, and Ireland, the eighteenth, and of Scotland the fifty-fourth. Anno Domini 1620.*

As one of the earliest immigrant vessels, the *Mayflower* ship has become a cultural icon in the history of the United States. The **Mayflower Compact** has also become an iconic piece of Americana.

A handful of men who were reasonably famous early settlers and/or searchers on Oak Island, Nova Scotia, had a direct connection to signers of the **Mayflower Compact** – a story for a future chapter of this book.

Of the 102 passengers on the *Mayflower*, there were 50 men, 19 women and 33 young adults and children. Just 41 of these were true Pilgrims, or religious separatists seeking freedom from the Church of England.

The others were considered common folk, including merchants, craftsmen, indentured servants and orphaned children. The Pilgrims called them "strangers."

The *Mayflower* landed on the coast of Cape Cod, in modern-day Massachusetts, on November 11, 1620.

Its target had been the area around the Hudson River, north of the still developing Virginia Colony, and hundreds of miles from where the *Mayflower* ended up.

The explanation passed down by the Pilgrims was that a serious storm had blown the *Mayflower* off course, and that they had arrived in America too late in the year to correct themselves.

It is a plausible explanation yet, according to one theory, many on the *Mayflower* had much to gain from their faulty navigation. Leaders of the group were seeking religious independence in America and, above all, a freedom from the corrupting influences that were ever-present in England and elsewhere.

They were not in close religious alignment with the Anglicans of Virginia, and may have justly feared that tensions and a loss of freedom might have arisen had they settled in that colony.

Other people had economic reasons to favor an isolated location. Many people on the *Mayflower* were bonded out to the London Company (of Virginia) for seven year terms of indentured servitude.

The London Company's jurisdiction included Virginia and some parts north, but it ended well short of Cape Cod. By remaining in the wrong place, these indentured servants were indentured no more, and could live on equal terms with the rest of the Pilgrims.

Whatever their reason for choosing the New England coast to settle, the passengers and crew withstood tremendous hardship, danger and death, not only from Nature, but from a few unfriendly Natives as well.

A level of at least some social equality was ensured by the **Mayflower Compact**, which was signed upon arrival by 41 adult male settlers on the *Mayflower*.

This compact has been interpreted as a precursor to American democratic ideals. This is part of a more general story of how the sacred values of the American Revolution and later periods had a genesis in 1620.

The fact of the matter is, the authority of King James was assumed to be God-given in the **Mayflower Compact**, and its "equal rights" nature in other areas was a practical necessity. With fewer than a hundred men present, the Pilgrim leaders could not afford to drive anyone away with autocratic overreach.

The Pilgrim colony nearly failed. It was to their great fortune that they had stumbled upon the ruins of an abandoned Native settlement.

Previous explorers had exposed the local Natives to a deathly plague, and Cape Cod was thereby fertile, yet almost unpopulated.

The once imprisoned Squanto had survived and joined others in providing guidance to the Pilgrims on their new environment.

There were some *Mayflower* passengers who died at sea from November 1620 through January 1621. On November 16, 1620, five days after land was spotted, William Butten, a youth and servant, died while the *Mayflower* waited at sea until the best spot could be found to make a settlement. Four passengers died onboard ship during December, and one died in Plymouth Harbor in January. These shipboard deaths were the very first deaths of the *Mayflower* company and were a precursor to several more deaths to come, many from the elements and others from diseases and scurvy.

By about mid-December 1620, it was decided that the company would settle at a location which was named Plymouth, and eventually all on the *Mayflower* moved ashore, where more deaths occurred.

Forty-five of the 102 *Mayflower* passengers died in the winter of 1620–21, and the *Mayflower* colonists suffered greatly during their first winter in the New World from lack of shelter and from scurvy. It would take nearly 150 years before the Western world learned that something as simple as sauerkraut could prevent scurvy.

In 1768, Captain James Cook was one of the first to trust in this theory and, three years after leaving England for the South Pacific with his store of Sour Kroutt (as it was then spelled), and with not a single death attributed to scurvy, Cook returned home to report his findings.

I can't help but imagine that the famous Oak Island cabbage farmer Samuel Ball may have made his fortune providing cabbage to be made into sauerkraut to prevent scurvy on ships that plied Nova Scotia's waters.

Scurvy and other hardships left the Plymouth Colony of *Mayflower* Pilgrims in a precarious position. As if all this wasn't enough, French forces were stationed at Port Royal, Nova Scotia, located on the western or leeward shore of what they called Acadia, and just a few days sail from Plymouth.

It wasn't known by the Puritans just how many French sailors and soldiers were at Port Royal, or in what state they could be found. It was enough to know that just a relatively short distance away Catholic Frenchmen could be dispatched against their Protestant counterparts, who would be found in dire straits and easily conquered.

At this point, Sir Ferdinando Gorges stepped in once again. Knowing that, by this time in history, Scottish mercenary forces had served on battlefields across Europe and the British Isles for centuries, Gorges approached his fellow Plymouth investor, Sir William Alexander, with the idea that he might settle Acadia with Scotsmen, as he drove the Catholic French either further into Canada, or even back to France.

Gorges also petitioned King James I to take action against the Acadian French at Port Royal.

James turned to William Alexander, his fellow Scot, to see if he could raise enough Scotsmen to go to what the French then called Acadia, or Acadie.

It is very possible that Gorges and Alexander conspired in a way that led King James to the idea of granting Acadia to Alexander. This land was originally, at least in Gorges's mind, part of his New England grant.

Dalhousie University is located in Halifax, Nova Scotia, about an hour from Oak Island. I have connected this university to Oak Island in a few different ways.

According to a 1922 *Dalhousie Review* article, it was:

> *Ferdinando Gorges, Governor of New Plymouth, through whose influence the charter rights of the New England Company over Acadia were surrendered to permit a re-grant of the lands to (William) Alexander.*

Sir William Alexander refers to his first connection with the Nova Scotia scheme in 1624 when writing:

> *Being much encouraged hereunto by Ferdinando Gorges and some others of the undertakers for New England, I showed them that my countrymen would never adventure in such an enterprise, unless it were, as there was a New France, a New Spain, and a New England, that they might likewise have a New Scotland.*

This was the very moment that the idea of creating Nova Scotia as a New Scotland was conceived, and the reason given was to protect the Plymouth Colony.

Without the *Mayflower* passengers hanging on for dear life at Plymouth, Gorges would have no reason to call for their protection. Without the protection provided by Sir William Alexander's attempt to colonize Acadia as New Scotland, or Nova Scotia, the French could have continued to build their strength in Acadia until they were able to oust the English from Plymouth, or worse.

These groups were interdependent and it can easily be surmised that each paid close attention to what was happening with the other.

We know this was the case for William Alexander as he ended up as proprietor of Cuttyhunk, the Elizabeth Islands, and even much of New York City. It appears to be the case for the New Englanders too, as they fought in years to come for English control of Nova Scotia.

Many men living within a one hundred mile radius of Plymouth, Massachusetts, also came to Oak Island to search for treasure, and/or to settle there.

And so it seems that the histories of each area were not kept secret from each other but, in fact, were shared in legends and traditions, in historical records, and in family genealogies.

Sir William had almost certainly been to North America by this point. In 1609 (the year he was knighted by King James), and again in 1611, Sir William received commissions to go to the general region surrounding and including the future Nova Scotia to look after the fur trading business that was being carried on there.

As early as 1624, he wrote, "I have never remembered anything with more admiration than America."

A July 25, 1626, letter written by King Charles I (who followed his father to the throne) mentions:

*A place in America commonly called by the name of Nova Scotia, already discovered and surveyed by the pains and travel of our well-beloved counsellor, Sir William Alexander of Menstrie.* (Menstrie Castle was Alexander's home in Scotland).

King James had already announced the proposal to settle Nova Scotia in a royal letter dated August 5, 1621, which reads:

*We have the more willingly harkened to a motion made to us by our trusty and well beloved Counsellour, Sir William Alexander, Knight, who hath a purpose to procure a foreign plantation of the lands lying between New England and Newfoundland.*

That purpose, at least on paper, was to protect the *Mayflower* settlers of the Plymouth Colony.

It is much more likely that William Alexander's intentions were to satisfy his own desire to be part of the settlement of the New World, and looked to Nova Scotia as nothing less than a utopia. He wrote this in a book, published in 1624, titled *An Encouragement To Colonies.*

Alexander speaks of his idyllic Nova Scotia, and he publishes a map that same year. On the map is the name of Ferdinando Gorges. Although Sir Francis Bacon also received a land grant in Newfoundland in 1611, there is no evidence that Bacon or Gorges ever made it to North America. But Sir William Alexander obviously did.

Many men and women were instrumental in the founding of Canada and the United States, but it can be fairly argued that, under the auspices of King James I of England and Ireland (King James VI of Scotland), three men stand out as enablers of the many brave people who made the earliest trips to the New World from the British Isles. These men, of course, were Sir Ferdinando Gorges, Sir William Alexander, and Sir Francis Bacon, as I have explained in this chapter.

The French had much earlier laid claim to Canada and to some extent New England. The first permanent French settlements in Canada were at Port Royal in 1605, and Quebec City in 1608, as fur trading posts.

Captain John Smith surveyed the coasts of Maine and the Massachusetts Bay and, in 1616, he named the region New England, claiming it for England.

A French leader named Claude de la Tour had already attempted a settlement in New England in the Penobscot Bay area of modern-day Maine. Fort Pentagouet, a trading post and fishing station that he built there in the winter of 1613, was abandoned about 1626, with Claude de la Tour sailing to France to secure arms and supplies to support Port Royal (which was soon to come under attack by the forces of Sir William Alexander).

Without the *Mayflower* settlement at Plymouth there would likely be no excuse for William Alexander to raise forces against the French at Port Royal, and to then establish the new colony of Nova Scotia. And so, the 400-year-old histories of these two significant places in North America are profoundly tied to one another.

*These three men were distinctly responsible for the settling of English speaking people in New England, and also in Nova Scotia, through their association with the Plymouth Colony and its Mayflower descendants.*

*Top right:*
*Sir Ferdinando Gorges*

*Center left:*
*Sir William Alexander*

*Bottom right:*
*Sir Francis Bacon*

*Chapter Two*

# MY OAK ISLAND THEORY

Beyond a few scattered trading posts, the year 1621 began with very few actual settlements in New England or Acadia (soon to be known as Nova Scotia).

The Pilgrims were suffering through a rough winter at Plymouth, while a contingent of French trappers and military men were stationed at Port Royal, Acadia. The next closest significant settlements were Quebec further west into Canada, Newfoundland to the north, and the struggling Virginia Colony much further to the south.

It was into this barren wilderness that Sir William Alexander was asking settlers, principally from Scotland, to begin a new life. Understandably, convincing people, despite their often meager conditions in the Old World, to pick up all they owned, leave family, friends, and the graves of their ancestors behind for a relatively unknown New World, would prove a difficult task.

At least some of the readers of this book will not be familiar with my Oak Island treasure theory, and others may need a refresher course. While it is important for me to repeat it here for context, I will try not to get into too much detail, as this book is intended to cover more of what happened after the events that I believe led up to the creation of the Money Pit on Oak Island.

My theory is pretty simple, although I have uncovered a large amount of supporting evidence for it. And, as they say, extraordinary claims require extraordinary proof. Here is the theory in a nutshell –

The followers of a group of Scottish knights settled in Nova Scotia during the early 1600s under Sir William Alexander, whom I introduced in the previous chapter.

This is a historic fact.

They were ousted by a treaty in the spring of 1632, and were unable to sail immediately across the North Atlantic because of extremely bad weather.

And so, 1632 is my target date for the Oak Island mystery to begin, when these folks were forced to bury some of their treasure and belongings on Oak Island.

Based on the families who later came there to settle or search, the evidence seems to show that the legend of a treasure buried somewhere on Oak Island stayed alive in three distinct groups of people:

• The descendants of the Knights Baronet of Nova Scotia, who were led by Sir William Alexander;

• The descendants of Freemasons, an organization which appears to have first begun with the initiation of William Alexander's two sons, William the younger and Anthony Alexander, who were initiated as the earliest known non-operative stonemasons, on July 3, 1634;

• The descendants of families either arriving on the *Mayflower* or moving into the area of Plymouth, Massachusetts, over the next century, most likely because Plymouth was the catalyst for William Alexander to receive Nova Scotia in the first place.

The proof of the second part of my theory lies in the vast percentage of early landowners and prominent searchers for treasure from these three groups, who came to Oak Island once it was safe to locate there.

On September 10, 1621, William Alexander received a charter for Nova Scotia. That charter would take about half a chapter to reproduce. However, borrowing from Alexander Fraser, who wrote an essay on the charter and the Knights Baronet of Nova Scotia, in 1922 –

*Alexander's intention with respect to the baronetcies was twofold; to make such a geographical distribution of the honours throughout Scotland as would embrace those rural parts in which, because of an excess in the population, the major portion of the emigrants ought to be available; and, also, to include members of noble families having considerable landed interests and prestige in that kingdom. Both these classes, it was believed, would naturally be best fitted to divert either migration or overpopulation to the new overseas Scottish colony.*

In other words, Alexander needed men to settle his new land, and he also needed leaders who could gather these men together for immigration and financially support them as cities and towns in Nova Scotia were being built. Scotland could provide both.

There are many indications that he, in fact, envisioned himself as King of Nova Scotia, and though listed as Lieutenant-General, Governor, Knight Admiral, etc., he was, in every sense of the word, the de facto King of Nova Scotia. And a king must have his knights.

Fraser, author of the previously mentioned essay, states: "The rights conferred by the charter have been considered powers of an almost *regal* nature."

In the article published in the *Dalhousie Review,* titled "Nova Scotia's Charter," Colonel Alexander Fraser, who was the Provincial Archivist for Ontario at the time, states of Sir William Alexander: "We have, in his case, an example of a poet, a philosopher, and an accomplished civil officer with *dreams of empire revolving in his mind.*"

Even earlier, in a document that declared all Knights Baronet of Nova Scotia to essentially be above the law, it is written that they should be governed only "by the laws of the said *Realm of Nova Scotia*... expressed in the investment granted to Sir William Alexander and his heirs..." The word realm is typically defined as a kingdom, and so this very real charter for the Knights Baronet of Nova Scotia is referring to that province as a *kingdom* under the control of Sir William Alexander.

Also, Joan Harris, a past owner of a mysterious stone foundation discovered at New Ross, Nova Scotia, stated that she was told by a First Nations member that his ancestors had helped build a "secret estate" for William Alexander, who was to be the *King of Nova Scotia.*

Further, Clan Donald had for centuries been thought of as a separate kingdom from Scotland, and now that Scotland had been absorbed into Great Britain, William Alexander MacDonald (his full name) may have seen this as a chance to revive the MacDonald Lordship of the Isles **kingdom** under his own leadership.

Sir William's partner Robert Gordon, at the time the premier Baronet of Nova Scotia, referred to Nova Scotia as a *kingdom* in his writings in 1625.

The book *Scotland Social and Domestic*, written in 1869 by Charles Rogers, states that William Alexander acquired the *"vice-sovereignty* of Nova Scotia," meaning he was second only to the king as sovereign there.

Oak Island author Mark Finnan, in his book *The First Nova Scotian*, states: "(King) James had been generous to his Master of Requests for Scotland (William Alexander), making him *virtual king* of a vast new domain."

One contemporary of Alexander, when referring to King James and William Alexander, wrote that: "A king who would be a poet, made a poet a *king*."

Another contemporary wrote a eulogy of sorts about William Alexander shortly after his death. Sir Thomas Urquhart penned a very unflattering bit of literature about William Alexander. Included in his writings is this: "*Like another King Arthur,* he (William Alexander) must have his knights, though nothing limited to so small a number; for how many soever that could have looked out for one day like gentlemen... they had a scale from him whereby to ascend unto platforms of virtue."

Urquhart continues: "Their *king* (William Alexander, again) nevertheless, not to stain his royal dignity, or seem to merit the imputations of selling honor to his subjects, did for their money give them land."

It seems that many contemporary and more modern day historians feel it was at least the secret ambition of William Alexander to become *King of Nova Scotia*.

With all the powers invested in Sir William, he was indeed the *de facto* King of Nova Scotia, and his "Plan B" may well have been to create his very own kingdom.

Alexander's first few years in the settlement of Nova Scotia went painfully slowly. He sent his first ship to Nova Scotia in 1622, however it was stranded by a storm in Newfoundland and never advanced further.

In 1623, William Alexander sent a second ship to Nova Scotia. It was named the *St. Luke* and it arrived at what is now called Port Mouton after following the Atlantic coastline of Nova Scotia and passing by Mahone Bay, and thereby Oak Island, twice.

The *St. Luke* left London, England, in March of 1623, but remained at Plymouth, England, on the western tip of the country, until better sailing weather arrived due to "contrary winds." Here, Ferdinando Gorges could look over the expedition that he helped inspire, while offering hospitality until fairer weather came along.

The *St. Luke* finally left Plymouth, England (as did the *Mayflower*), on April 28th, reaching Newfoundland on June 5th, "having no good winds at all."

These adventurers found that the crew from the 1622 ship had dispersed and their blacksmith and minister (the only two non-sailors they could convince to go with them) were both dead. Ten men from the first ship joined with the crew of the 1623 ship to continue the journey.

The *St. Luke* carried some settlers who attempted a colony in the area of Port Mouton, Nova Scotia, which was, at the time, called Port de Mutton, gaining this name when a sheep fell off a French ship into the bay.

On June 23rd, they left Newfoundland but were wrapped in fog for 14 days, finally seeing the west coast of Cape Breton on July 8th, and then continued to sail down the Atlantic coast until July 13th.

They passed Port Mouton and, according to Sir William's own account, explored: "three very pleasant harbours, and (going) ashore on one of them, which after their ship's name, they called St. Luke's Bay."

Even though it has commonly been said that they renamed Port de Mutton Bay as St. Luke's Bay, they were actually about fourteen miles down the coast.

In fact, they were almost certainly at the bay formed by the Sable River. It is worth noting that the head of land at the opening of that bay is still called Louis Head, which could conceivably have come from Luke's Head, since they named the bay St. Luke's Bay and a broader area further inland as Luckesburgh or Luke's Borough, as shown on a map Alexander first published in 1624.

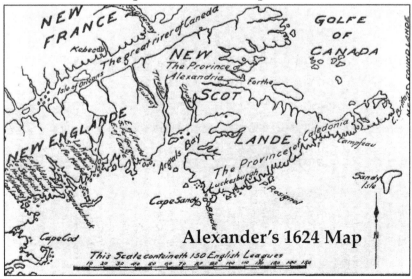

**Alexander's 1624 Map**

In this enlargement of a section of William Alexander's map can be seen Sir Ferdinando Gorges's name just next to the Earl of Arundel (the man who oversaw the trial of Sir Francis Bacon). See arrow 1.

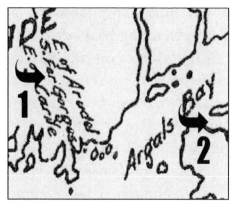

Arrow 2 points to the approximate location of Port Royal, home to a French contingent soon to be ousted by William Alexander's men. Argals Bay, on this map, is now the Bay of Fundy, home to the highest tides in the world, typically peaking at about 50 feet.

At least three families have legends maintaining that William Alexander had an "estate" built at New Ross, about 20 miles above Oak Island, in 1623. This could have been a beachhead from which to spy on the French located about 60 miles directly overland at Port Royal.

It is an Alexander family legend that, in 1625, a grandson named John was born to William Alexander at the "Alexander estate in Nova Scotia."

The Alexander clan has a family history stating that at least some of the family remained at New Ross, NS, until their estate was burned down by Oliver Cromwell's men in 1654, which fits well with Nova Scotia history.

It is known that the Puritan Robert Sedgwick, Major General of Massachusetts, invaded Nova Scotia in 1654 to conquer any and all enemies of Oliver Cromwell.

There is more to be told of Robert Sedgwick.

Something else very big was happening in 1622-1623. This is part of my theory, but again I don't want to delve too deeply into it here so that I can stay on track with the *Mayflower*/Oak Island connection.

Very quickly, a man named Alexander (Al) Strachan began plotting in 1622 to rob perhaps the richest man in Scotland, George Keith, the Earl Marischal or top law enforcement officer in Scotland.

The Marischal's position was hereditary and George's family was able to build up a vast fortune. He was also married to a woman 30 years younger than he was.

In early 1623, Strachan robbed not only the treasure of George Keith, but also his younger wife. George died in April 1623, and not too long afterward Al Strachan and the former Mrs. Keith were married.

I scoured my contacts in Scotland and any records I could find on my own. There is no indication where the bulk of this treasure ended up, although the record is clear as to what items made up the treasure, and that Strachan was indicted for the crime.

Strachan's trial was postponed a few times and, by 1625, shortly before the Knights Baronet of Nova Scotia were created by William Alexander (under the auspices of King James), Strachan received a full pardon for his crime. Shortly thereafter, he became the third Knight Baronet of Nova Scotia, and a partner of Alexander, under Charles I, son of James (who died March 27th).

Strachan even signed as witness to a 1630 charter granted to Claude de la Tour, the French leader who left behind his trading post in New England in 1626.

This 1630 charter, issued by William Alexander to Claude de la Tour, and witnessed by Alexander Strachan, involved a bit of territory that may have included Oak Island, or at least land that was located very close to it. I'll discuss this further as the story develops.

The first concrete action towards the establishment of the Knights Baronet of Nova Scotia in 1625 involved just four men - Sir William Alexander, Al Strachan, who stole the Keith family treasure, William Keith, who would have inherited that very treasure, and Robert Gordon, a special military intelligence agent for King James.

Alexander had struggled to raise the funding he needed for Nova Scotia. Likewise, according to the official minutes of the king's Privy Council, the 1620s were a time of severe financial hardship for King James, and he was openly demanding that loans be made to him under penalty of the law. This was particularly true in 1622 and 1623, when the Strachan robbery was being planned and carried out.

This tells me that the fix was in to steal this massive treasure in order to fund Nova Scotia, so that its wealth in furs, lumber and precious metals could, in turn, improve the king's fortunes, while satisfying William Alexander's desire to create his own kingdom.

In 1628, William Alexander the younger, son of Sir William Alexander, led a small fleet of ships to Nova Scotia. It is often said that they must have stayed somewhere besides Nova Scotia that first winter, as they did not take Port Royal from the French until the following year.

However, there is contemporary writing that seems to indicate that they may have made it to Nova Scotia that year, just not to Port Royal. Historians have never been able to pin down exactly where these Scottish settlers stayed during the winter of 1628.

On November 18, 1628, William Alexander, Sr., wrote a letter to William Graham, Earl of Mentieth, who held the position of the highest court justice in all of Scotland. In this letter, Alexander states: "My sone, praised be God, is returned safe, having left a colonie neare Canada behind him, and I am dealing for a new setting forth from London." It is highly doubtful that this letter would have been a lie or a forgery, but it should be noted that he only says, "neare Canada," not "at Port Royal."

A few days later, however, Sir John Maxwell, Knight Baronet of Nova Scotia, writes to his brother William Maxwell: "It is for certaintie that Sir William Alexander (the younger) is come home again from Nova Scotia..."

Again, no specific mention of Port Royal is made, and I think it is at least possible that the 1628 settlers remained at New Ross, their ships anchored in Mahone Bay, while William the younger returned to England.

Regardless of the exact date of arrival at Port Royal, Nova Scotia, the Scots were firmly entrenched there by 1629, and built a fort called Charles Fort, after King Charles I, who by now had succeeded his father, King James I, who died shortly after the Knights Baronet of Nova Scotia title was created, but a few months before the first of these honors were given out to Strachan and the others.

For the next three years, from 1629 through 1632, more ships came to Port Royal bringing settlers and supplies. There is an old legend that the number of people at Port Royal, during this period, may have reached as many as 2,000 at one point, if the crews of arriving ships were included.

Fate would step in to tear apart the plans of Sir William Alexander and of the many Knights Baronet who had invested their money and their followers in this dream of America, and particularly in Nova Scotia.

The King of England and the King of France were brothers-in-law. France owed the English King Charles I half of a dowry promised to him when he married the French king's sister. In return for full payment of the dowry, Charles agreed to return Nova Scotia to the French. However, at the same time, Charles was telling anxious Knights Baronet of Nova Scotia, and William Alexander, that he was not giving up on Nova Scotia.

Historical records show that the Port Royal Scots were told to leave at the end of March 1632, but did not reach Great Britain until June. They had to have stayed somewhere for two to three months, and I believe they took shelter in Mahone Bay, where one of their vessels sunk. I believe they anchored near Oak Island, where they buried what they couldn't take back with them, including the stolen Strachan treasure, with the idea that someday they would return to retrieve it.

However, the French took over Nova Scotia, and Oliver Cromwell's movement took over Great Britain, leaving these people between a rock and a hard place.

I believe legends of the treasure were kept alive in the three groups of people I've identified, who were all aware of the original settlement attempt. Once the British came back to Nova Scotia in full force, families from these three groups – Knights Baronet, Freemasons, and Plymouth Colony (or nearby) residents – descended on Oak Island as landowners and as treasure hunters.

I think that a cache of treasure and other goods was buried on Oak Island sometime between April and June of 1632, with the idea that this was simply a bump in the road for the Knights Baronet settlement of Nova Scotia.

Gilbert Hedden, an owner and searcher for treasure on Oak Island, gave the dates of about 1630 and as far back as 1635, in letters he wrote – one to Franklin Delano Roosevelt and one to another Oak Island fan.

Coincidentally, the halfway point of these two years would actually be the end of June, 1632, matching my date very closely.

Hedden, along with Les MacPhie and Graham Harris, all engineers, and all students of the Oak Island mystery, agree that the Money Pit could have been constructed in about three months with a small group of men. Hedden stated this in a letter, and MacPhie and Harris wrote this in their book, *Oak Island And Its Lost Treasure*.

From what I understand, Hedden arrived at his date of the early 1630s using mapping and surveying techniques. I arrived at my date of 1632 using historical documents. However, there are several carbon dating records and artifacts which also point to the early 1600s as a time of great activity on Oak Island.

For instance, a piece of axe cut wood was found deep in the ground near the Money Pit which dated to as old as 1626. Another significant piece of wood found in the eye of the swamp dated to as old as 1619. A wetlands specialist, Dr. Ian Spooner, stated that there is evidence of substantial work in the swamp in the early 1600s.

Other carbon dating records belonging to Fred Nolan, Dan Blankenship, and the current team of searchers, show dates that could also fit my 1632 date.

In addition, two shoes found in the mud off a sunken wharf date to before 1700 based on their construction, as do some of the forged nails found at Smith's Cove, based on the amount of carbon found in the steel.

A piece of ship's planking found in the Oak Island swamp dated into the 1600s, as did a pair of scissors from Smith's Cove, located near the famous Oak Island Money Pit.

A piece of red stoned jewelry was estimated to be 400 to 500 years old based on the hand cut nature of the gem, and also human bones, found at great depth in the area of the Money Pit, dated to as early as the 1600s.

It's even been said that a sunken ship built about 1600 lies within sight of Oak Island.

Items dating to the later 1600s and early 1700s may have been left behind by people searching for the treasure.

I believe this is the case with a 1671 knighthood medallion found at New Ross, which I will further explain, and also likely the case for some King Charles II coins also found on Oak Island.

In fact, I think that searches were being conducted for the Oak Island treasure long before the Money Pit depression was found in 1795. I have read articles that point to at least 25 years before, and up to 100 years before. I believe that searches for the Oak Island treasure took place whenever possible and safe, beginning not too long after the treasure was buried.

I have plenty more information and potential proof of my theory in my previous books, which rated #6 out of the Top 25 on *The Curse of Oak Island* TV show in 2019.

New England was also seeing considerable activity during this time period – 1621 through 1632.

Sir Ferdinando Gorges first created Lygonia in the southern area of what became the State of Maine, which is likely represented by his name appearing on William Alexander's 1624 map.

The first European settlement in the area was actually made on St. Croix Island in 1604 by a French party that included Samuel de Champlain. After a rough winter, the French moved over to Port Royal in 1605.

French and English forces would contest ownership of Nova Scotia and New England until 1763, when the French were defeated in the French and Indian War.

English colonists, being sponsored by the Plymouth Company, founded a settlement in Maine in 1607 (the Popham Colony at Phippsburg), but it was abandoned the following year.

In 1613, a French trading post was established at present-day Castine, Maine, by Claude de la Tour, which he abandoned in 1626.

The territory between the Merrimack and Kennebec rivers was first called the Province of Maine in a 1622 land patent granted to Sir Ferdinando Gorges and his friend John Mason. The two split the territory along the Piscataqua River in a 1629 pact that resulted in the Province of New Hampshire being formed by Mason in the south, and New Somersetshire being created by Gorges to the north, in what is now southwestern Maine.

One of the first English attempts to settle the Maine coast was by Christopher Levett, an agent for Gorges and a member of the Plymouth Council for New England. After securing a royal grant for 6,000 acres of land on the site of present-day Portland, Maine, Levett built a stone house and left a group of men behind.

He returned to England in 1623, to drum up support for his settlement, which he called York after the city of his birth in England.

Levett's settlement, like the Popham Colony, also failed, and the men that Levett left behind were never heard from again. Levett did sail back across the Atlantic to meet with Massachusetts Bay Colony governor, John Winthrop, at Salem in 1630, but died on the return voyage without ever returning to his settlement.

The New Somersetshire colony was small and, in 1639, Gorges received a second patent from Charles I covering the same territory as Gorges's 1629 settlement with Mason. Gorges's second effort resulted in the establishment of more settlements along the coast of southern Maine and along the Piscataqua River.

A dispute over the bounds of another land grant led to the short-lived formation of Lygonia on territory that encompassed a large area of the Gorges grant. Both Gorges's Province of Maine and Lygonia had been absorbed into the Massachusetts Bay Colony by 1658.

Later in history, on June 19, 1819, the Massachusetts General Court separated the District of Maine from the rest of the Commonwealth of Massachusetts.

Ferdinando Gorges's land, in what became Maine, was located across from Port Royal, Nova Scotia. He wasn't alone. Al Strachan also received a charter for land in what is now New Brunswick (originally part of the Nova Scotia grant), which was also across the bay from Port Royal. Strachan's Knights Baronet charter reads:

> *Granted under the Great Seal in favour of Sir Alexander Straquhan of Thornetoune, now a baronet of all and whole a great part or portion of land in the province and lordship of Nova Scotia in America which was particularly bounded and limited, as follows: In the first, a great southern part of land or promontory on the east side of the river now Clyde, called Prince Saint John, and then proceeding west for three miles to the seashore and from there proceeding north to the seashore on land on the west side of the said river, always observing three miles in latitude, extending to the number of 16,000 acres of land.*

This land was located not near the current Clyde River of Nova Scotia, but rather in New Brunswick near the St. John River.

This location is important for three reasons.

First, it was strategically located across the Bay of Fundy from Port Royal, just as Ferdinando Gorges's grant was further south in present day Maine.

Second, this was the general location of a trading post later established by Charles de la Tour, son of Claude de la Tour, who has been mentioned a few times earlier in this book.

Third, a lead cross was found near this location which matches fairly closely to a lead cross found on Oak Island by the Lagina team. Archaeologists believe that the tiny lead cross discovered in Saint John dates all the way back to the settlement of the nearby provincial historic site of Fort La Tour from the 17th century.

The cross on the black background was found in 2019 in New Brunswick. The cross on the gray background was found on Oak Island in 2018.

Although these crosses are similar but not identical, it is at least interesting that they were both found at locations associated with William Alexander, Al Strachan and the La Tour family.

It is unknown if Al Strachan ever set foot on his St. John land. However, Charles de la Tour, son of Claude, later had a trading post there.

William Alexander issued the two charters of land involved – one to Al Strachan, and the other to Claude and his son Charles de la Tour.

Al Strachan witnessed the charter that either included Oak Island, or at least came very near to it, and was himself the recipient of the St. John grant.

Charles de la Tour had been considered an equal partner in his father's grant near Oak Island, but refused to accept it. Not too far into the future he moved to St. John where he set up his trading post.

That all three families were involved in both locations where these crosses were found at least warrants a closer look.

It can be easily seen that the histories of Nova Scotia, New Brunswick, and the New England states of Maine, Massachusetts, Connecticut and New Hampshire were intricately tied to one another during this early part of their development.

The reader should not get lost in the idea that what was happening in Nova Scotia had nothing to do with what was happening in New England. One was tied to the other right up until the early settlement of Oak Island and the early searches that took place there.

The bit of land I've referred to a few times now as including Oak Island, or at least being very near to Oak Island, was recorded as Mirliguesche, or sometimes Mirligaiche. Oak Island historian Doug Crowell first got me started looking into the true location of this piece of land and its name origin.

Why this matters is that it was the northeasternmost extent of Claude de la Tour's land, and also of the land of Thomas Temple, whose story sorely needs to be told.

(As a tease, Sir Thomas Temple was a substantial sponsor of Harvard University, and appears to be a forefather of two very important people in the history of treasure hunting on Oak Island. I'll get to him soon.)

The oldest known writing of Mirliguesche was in the 1630 charter that William Alexander granted to Claude de la Tour and his son, Charles.

Credit is sometimes given to French commander Isaac de Razilly for naming Mirliguesche, but he couldn't have, since he didn't reach Nova Scotia until two years after the La Tour grant. Mirliguesche is also, at times, given as a Native name, and said to only refer to the town of Lunenburg, which is situated near Oak Island.

The spellings of Mirliguesche and Mirligaiche seem to have been interchangeable and were each used by both French and English writers.

Sylvie Delorme was helping translate a document from French to English for Oak Island researcher Doug Crowell. In the process, she noticed that the Mirligaiche spelling had a similarity to the Gaelic language, and so Doug contacted me to see what I could discover.

What I discovered was that the word Mirligaiche was an ancient Gaelic term for "a part of an alliance."

Beyond the 1630 deed, the next oldest mention on an official document appears to be a French map, shown below, which comes from a journal written in 1684 concerning a French exploration down the Atlantic coastline of Nova Scotia.

On this map, Mirligaiche is mentioned three times.

Number 1 is in the paragraph where "La Baye de Mirligaiche," or "The Bay of Mirligaiche," is mentioned. Number 2 is in the center of the bay where "B. (or bay) de Mirligaich" (sic) is written. Finally, at number 3, in an upside-down position, we see written "La Pointe de Mirligaiche," or "The Point of Mirligaiche."

The journal is described as a – "Manuscript journal, detailing an expedition along the Atlantic Coast of Nova Scotia and parts of New Brunswick situated on the Bay of Fundy, July 19, 1684." Dalhousie University states that the accompanying journal map refers to "Mahone Bay, called here Mirligaiche."

I straightened the north-south direction of the map and placed it over a modern day map of Mahone Bay, with only slight adjustments.

The two maps coincide, as shown below.

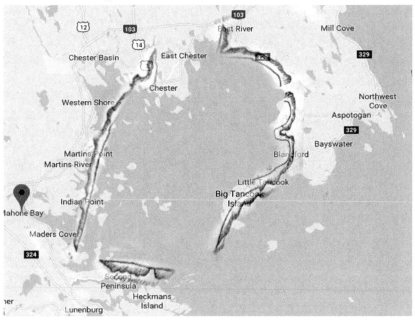

Mirligaiche is mentioned again in *Le Grand Dictionnaire Géographique* (1768) as being "full of islands." Lunenburg Bay has very few islands. It may be a matter of semantics or misunderstanding, but it appears that I am not the only person who has believed that Mirligaiche included Mahone Bay, and thus Oak Island.

*Chapter Three*

# LA TOUR, TEMPLE AND PHIPS

In this chapter I will address the history of three men who, in one way or another, served as governors of Nova Scotia: Charles de la Tour, whose father, Claude, once had a trading post in modern-day New England; Thomas Temple, who later became a prominent and important citizen of Boston, Massachusetts, and financial supporter of Harvard University; and William Phips, governor of the Province of Massachusetts Bay, which at the time included the Massachusetts Bay Colony, the Plymouth Colony, the Province of Maine, Martha's Vineyard, Nantucket, Nova Scotia, and New Brunswick.

Phips also came to Nova Scotia hunting for "plunder both by land and water, and also underground."

Another thing these three men had in common was that they were all knighted. I believe the knighthood medallion found at New Ross, dated 1671, was given to Phips as part of an honorary knighthood granted to him because of the large treasure that he recovered from the Spanish galleon *Concepción*. Most of the treasure ended up in the hands of King James II, and Phips's financier Christopher Monck, who was first given this medallion, according to information I discovered with help from the British Museum and many other significant people.

Governors Charles de la Tour and Thomas Temple were both knighted in the form of receiving the Knights Baronet of Nova Scotia title.

La Tour was knighted by King Charles I as part of his alliance with William Alexander. Thomas Temple was knighted by Charles II, son of Charles I, as part of his assumption of the governorship of Nova Scotia.

Before I get into the stories of these men, I need to explain a few events that predate their role as governors of Nova Scotia.

As of 1630, Sir William Alexander granted the land of Mirligaiche to Claude de la Tour and his son, Charles.

Whether this was the reason for naming the area as Mirligaiche, which in Gaelic means "a part of an alliance," or if it had already been named this, the important thing to know is that Charles de la Tour would not at first accept his portion of the land, or the title of Knight Baronet of Nova Scotia that came along with it.

In 1630, William Alexander the younger returned to Nova Scotia in two man-of-war ships containing supplies and settlers, with Claude de la Tour onboard.

The elder La Tour had been captured by Alexander's allies, the Kirke brothers, as he attempted to return to Port Royal with supplies for the French living there. He was taken to England where he decided to ally himself with William Alexander instead, in return for a large grant of land that extended from Mirligaiche to the southern cape of Nova Scotia. Upon his return, he attempted to persuade his son to follow in his footsteps and accept the title and the land. However, Charles de la Tour refused.

The father and son La Tours actually fought a two-day battle over this, with each deciding to go their separate ways, while maintaining at least an appearance of peace between them after the battle.

While in England, Claude had married his third wife, some say a close relative of Sir William Alexander, perhaps William's own sister.

Claude and his new wife took up lodging not far from his son's fort at Port La Tour, near the southernmost part of Nova Scotia. There is no indication that either one of the La Tour men ever set foot on Oak Island, but they may well have held the title to it if Mirligaiche included Oak Island as part of the alliance grant.

It could be fairly said that Native tribes first owned all of Nova Scotia (which would also include Oak Island) until the claim made by the French about 1604. There has been no trace of Native culture found on the island.

The French would then own Oak Island as part of their Acadia claim. There have been only a few tenuous finds on Oak Island attributed to the French.

With the claim made for Nova Scotia, in 1621, William Alexander would have clearly owned Oak Island.

I am not the first author who has hinted at Sir William Alexander having something to do with the beginning of the Oak Island mystery. Five other authors have dropped hints about him being somehow involved, and a sixth, more recent author has provided some evidence of a 17th century beginning to the Oak Island mystery.

However, I am the only author to lay out a complete theory of how Sir William Alexander was involved.

Alexander granted Mirligaiche to Claude de la Tour and his son in 1630, and so, if Mirligaiche included Oak Island, which I believe it did, they would be the first individual people ever named as owning the island, whether they ever set foot there or not.

I doubt seriously that they did.

By 1632, as the Scots were being forced out of Port Royal, Mirligaiche likely sat as pretty much unspoiled wilderness, except for a possible secret estate built for the Alexander family at New Ross.

The Scots were told to leave on March 29th, just a few days after the New Year of that era, which happened on March 25th.

In my *Oak Island Knights* book, and my *Oak Island Endgame* book, I make the case for why I believe they chose Mahone Bay in which to take shelter during the dangerous early spring weather of the North Atlantic.

I think one of their ships may have sunk in Mahone Bay, and I believe this led to them depositing some of their belongings, especially the treasure stolen by Al Strachan, on Oak Island, somewhat out of desperation and somewhat as a cache to be recovered as soon as fate would allow.

I don't intend to go into this theory much further as it would use up a lot of space in this book, which is intended, instead, to link the Plymouth Colony to Oak Island.

However, my theory has been discussed at length in the Oak Island "war room" and, as previously noted, it was ranked #6 out of the top 25 theories.

Suffice it to say that William Alexander found himself between a rock and a hard place as of 1632.

The French were now soundly in control of Nova Scotia, Alexander had lost a small personal fortune on the settlement attempt, and he now had many Knights Baronet of Nova Scotia breathing down his neck either for answers as to what the future held or to get their money back.

Alexander never did have enough personal wealth to take on the Nova Scotia settlement and now his family's fortunes were suffering severely.

In 1631, Charles I had granted him exclusive rights to publish the *Psalms of King David As Translated by King James* (translated with considerable help from Alexander).

You may recall that King James was responsible for the printing of the *King James Bible*, which brought the printed word to the masses.

Alexander helped with the *Psalms* translation as a separate project, and he now at least held exclusive rights to them. However, the printing of the *Psalms* in 1631, and again in 1637, brought little relief to his finances.

Having been named Secretary of State for Scotland for life, William Alexander still had some power. He used it to get his son Anthony appointed as Master of (Public) Works for Scotland.

A dustup with William Sinclair of Rosslyn over who should control the stonemason lodges of Scotland led to Anthony Alexander being accepted as one of the world's first known "non-operative" Masons, or what we would today refer to as a Freemason.

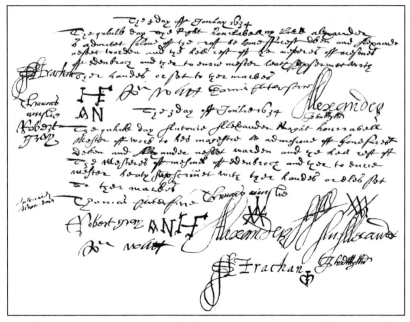

The above 1634 document is said to still be held by the Edinburgh Lodge #1 of Freemasonry. I found this copy in the official history of this lodge where I also found the Al Strachan treasure story. This book was dedicated to the leader of the Scottish Freemasons, whose uncle founded Dalhousie University, located just an hour from Oak Island. This is another story I will tell in a later chapter.

As the above document records, on July 3, 1634, William Alexander the younger was initiated as the first known non-operative Mason. Anthony was second, and Al Strachan was third.

In my previous books I show how all of the earliest of Scottish Freemasons were directly connected to the Knights Baronet of Nova Scotia, and so it is only logical that Freemasons would have developed a strong interest in what might be buried on Oak Island.

Without going too deeply into the details of why both the Freemasons and members of the families of the Knights Baronet of Nova Scotia might have a long-standing interest in Oak Island, I will, for now, point out that many of the searchers and landowners on Oak Island were Freemasons, and a few were actual descendants of Knights Baronet.

I'll address some of these people before returning to the *Mayflower* / Oak Island connections.

In two cases these men were collateral relatives of Sir William Alexander and his partner Al Strachan. All the word "collateral" means, in this usage, is that they were of the same family, but a description of their exact relationship would be too long and confusing to list.

Simply put, John Monro, an early landowner on Oak Island, was from the same family as Robert Monro, the son-in-law of William Alexander. Of interest is the fact that Robert Monro had been captured and put in prison by George Monck, the father of Christopher Monk.

You may remember that it was Christopher Monck who financed Sir William Phips's recovery of treasure from the Spanish ship *Concepción*.

It was also Christopher Monck who was first given the 1671 knighthood medallion that was found at New Ross back in the 1970s, and shown in the war room to Rick Lagina, Doug Crowell and I.

There were only three of these medallions issued in 1671. The location and ownership of the other two medallions has been proven beyond question. Therefore, the New Ross medallion had to once belong to Monck.

Photo by Elizabeth McQuiston

In the above photo, Rick Lagina, Doug Crowell and I are in the war room taking a look at the New Ross medallion. This was the first and only time it was ever shown in public, beyond close friends and family.

It appears the New Ross medallion and the other two were commemorative medals given out at the initiation of the three men knighted in 1671, but that they were exclusive to these men, and not given to others as tokens. This agrees with the British Museum description.

I discussed this medallion a few times with the curator of medals and coins of the British Museum. Their website states that: "It has been *erroneously* supposed that these medals were tickets of admission to the ceremony of the installation."

In addition to the New Ross medallion, the British Museum holds one of the other two 1671 medallions. The third was held by the Gustavianum Museum in Sweden until it was stolen and melted down.

I spoke with the staff at both of these museums to finally determine that the third medallion could have only belonged originally to Christopher Monck.

I also spoke to Thomas Woodcock, 'Garter Principal King of Arms,' who handles all official administration of this knighthood, and meets regularly with the Queen of England and with many other highly-placed people.

His exact words ending a much longer email were: "They appear to be commemorative medals; there is no reason why this third one might not have belonged to the Duke of Albemarle (Christopher Monck)."

In other words, since the other two have been historically connected specifically with King Charles of Sweden (the melted medallion) and to John of Saxony (the medallion held by the British Museum), there is no reason not to connect this last one specifically to Christopher Monck, the third and last Order of the Garter Knighthood recipient from 1671.

George Monck, father of Christopher Monck, fought beside Oliver Cromwell in 1650, and was responsible for the capture of David Alexander, who had captained one of the two privateer ships that accompanied William Alexander's son and settlers to Nova Scotia in 1628.

In 1654, after executing a military campaign against royalist rebels in the Highlands of Scotland, George Monck became Governor of Scotland at the behest of Oliver Cromwell.

This is the same year that the Alexander family was forced out of their estate at New Ross, Nova Scotia, by Cromwell's troops, when it was burned to the ground.

Oddly enough, James Monck, a great grandson of George, was on Oak Island in 1753 as a "surveyor," and yet Oak Island wasn't officially surveyed until 1762.

I recently discovered an entirely new link of George Monck to this story – he actually arrested Sir William Alexander's son-in-law, Robert Monro.

John Monro appears as an early landowner on Oak Island and his name is listed on this tax record between two well-known Oak Island 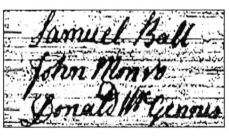 names: Samuel Ball and Donald McGinnis.

I traced John Monro's roots in my *Oak Island Endgame* book, where I detail his connection to the family of Robert Monro, son-in-law of William Alexander.

It seems more than coincidental that you would have a collateral relative of William Alexander living on Oak Island, but this is not even the half of it.

Doug Crowell told me that a man named John Strachan owned the Nolan Cross lots on Oak Island from 1841 through January of 1857, at the same time that the Truro Company was searching for treasure on Oak Island.

Again, I traced John Strachan's roots and he is also related to Al Strachan, the man who stole the treasure and the man who witnessed the Mirligaiche deed.

It seems perhaps beyond coincidence that relatives of both William Alexander and Al Strachan would be landowners on Oak Island. The coincidence expands beyond belief as we look at all the other landowners and searchers on Oak Island that had direct connections to our three specific groups of Freemasons, Knights Baronet of Nova Scotia, and Plymouth Colony residents.

Upon the death of Oliver Cromwell, a newly-elected British Parliament was to eventually invite Charles II to return to Britain as king with help from George Monck. For his services in contributing to a peaceful restoration of Stuart rule, George Monck was made the Duke of Albemarle and a Knight of the Order of the Garter. He was also awarded a large annual pension.

This same dignity of Knight of the Order of the Garter was bestowed on Monck's son, Christopher. It was his Order of the Garter medallion from 1671 that was found in the dirt "just a stone's throw away" from the mysterious New Ross foundation, as described by one of the finders of the medallion. It could only be a medallion given to Christopher Monck, based on my research. My theory of how it got to New Ross involves William Phips, which I will soon explain.

Another Knight Baronet family was represented on Oak Island by an early landowner Hector MacLean, uncle to John Smith. Smith purchased the Money Pit lot after he, Anthony Vaughan and Daniel McGinnis found indications that something was buried there. Hector appears to have been 7th in line of the MacLean Knights Baronet (as discussed in my *Oak Island Endgame* book).

I believe Smith, McGinnis, Vaughan, MacLean and even William Phips, were searching for a treasure they had heard about through family traditions and legends.

The same, I believe, held true for many other Oak Island landowners and treasure seekers, from Franklin Roosevelt to the Chappells, from Fred Blair to Simeon Lynds, and many more – some with links to Plymouth.

Tragedies struck the Alexander family, one after another, in the late 1630s. In 1637, Anthony Alexander, just about the time he was finally declared the sole Master of Works for Scotland (despite the protest of William Sinclair of Rosslyn) was found dead, with no reason given. Sinclair then urged the king to grant him the title of Master of Works, but instead King Charles gave the position to another Alexander (Henry), who became the world's seventh known non-operative Mason.

Anthony died September 17, 1637. The following year, almost eight months to the day, William Alexander the younger died on May 18, 1638. It is typically said that he died in Great Britain but some in the Alexander family say he died in Nova Scotia. A brother, Robert Alexander, died that same year, at the age of just twenty-five.

Another brother, John, is said by the Alexander family to have faked his own death and escaped to New Ross, where his family lived until 1654 when Cromwell's men burned down their estate. The family left for Virginia about 1656, where they founded Alexandria, Virginia.

Since so many sons appear to have died in a very short period of time, I've wondered if more of them actually faked their deaths and found sanctuary in Nova Scotia during a very trying time for the Alexander family.

A young grandson of William Alexander, destined to become William Alexander III, Earl of Stirling, is said to have died in 1640, followed shortly by a disheartened and penniless Sir William Alexander. It is further stated that his creditors were so upset with Sir William that they "arrested" his corpse and had it buried on the spot.

Claude de la Tour had also passed away by this point (dying sometime during or just after 1636) leaving the Knight Baronet title and ownership of the Mirligaiche grant in a state of limbo, and leaving Oak Island quiet and lonely, at least for the time being.

Charles de la Tour, having rejected his involvement in the Knights Baronet scheme, moved to St. John (now in New Brunswick), where he built a trading post. The French leader Isaac de Razilly came to Nova Scotia to take over as governor in late 1632. Oddly enough, rather than move directly to Port Royal (where the French had earlier settled, and where there were at least the remnants of buildings and plowed, fertile fields), he made his headquarters at LaHave, Nova Scotia, located only about 28 miles from Oak Island, and just 45 miles from New Ross.

Razilly's decision to set up headquarters at LaHave has never been fully understood, unless he wanted to be near where he may have heard that some type of treasure was buried. Razilly died suddenly at LaHave, Nova Scotia, in December 1635.

Claude de la Tour passed away most likely during the following year.

By 1640 there was virtually no one left alive that was involved in the Scots settlement attempt.

The only two principals left from that era were John Alexander (and his family), said to be living at New Ross, and Charles de la Tour (and his family), who had moved his trading operation to St. John in present-day New Brunswick, near land once owned by Al Strachan.

One of Razilly's lieutenants was Charles de Menou d'Aulnay, who was instrumental in maintaining the shipping to and from France.

Also, d'Aulnay took on military tasks such as ordering the capture of Fort Pentagouet on the Penobscot Bay, located in present-day Maine.

D'Aulnay could not oust Charles de la Tour from his leadership position in what the French were again calling Acadia. Instead, the two men became co-governors of sorts. The military forces of the two rivals were almost equal. D'Aulnay simply could not conquer La Tour.

In the early winter of 1641, d'Aulnay returned to France to obtain additional power, and La Tour sought the aid of his New England neighbors.

As a result of negotiations with New England's Governor Thomas Dudley (who had succeeded the famous Governor John Winthrop), a body of Boston merchants made a visit to Fort La Tour for purposes of trade. Upon their return, while still at sea, they met d'Aulnay himself, who informed them that La Tour was a rebel, and showed them confirmation of an order issued a year before for his arrest.

With 500 men in armed ships, d'Aulnay laid siege to Fort La Tour; but aid came from New England and he was driven away.

In 1645, learning that La Tour had taken a journey to Quebec, d'Aulnay again laid siege to Fort La Tour, but Madame de la Tour directed from the bastions a blistering cannon attack on the enemy's ships, and compelled d'Aulnay to retreat from the battle.

With the aid of a treacherous sentry, he was enabled, on his third attack, to enter the fort. But the resistance led by Madame de la Tour was so fierce that he proposed terms of surrender, pledging life and liberty to all in the garrison. His terms being accepted, d'Aulnay broke his agreement, hanging every member of the garrison, and forcing Madame de la Tour to witness the executions with a rope around her own neck. She died a few weeks later while her husband took refuge in Quebec.

D'Aulnay now had the whole of Acadia to himself. In 1645, he went to France, and received honors from the king. In 1647, a commission was issued making him governor and lieutenant-general of Acadia. However, he would not have much time to enjoy his triumph because he died in 1650 following a boating accident, throwing the governorship of Nova Scotia again into question.

Charles de la Tour, discovering the devastation made in his absence, immediately on his return from Quebec sailed for France. He laid the facts before the court and not only secured a restoration of his title and privileges, but also was made d'Aulnay's successor.

D'Aulnay's widow, Jeanne Motin, was still living in Nova Scotia with her children, and was alarmed at the turn these affairs had taken. Preparations, offensively and defensively, were made but all hostilities suddenly ceased. The leaders of the opposing forces, Charles de la Tour and Jeanne Motin d'Aulnay, decided to end their troubles by getting married to each other on February 24th, 1653. Peace seemed to have finally come to the land. But not for long.

Robert Sedgwick, a Puritan, merchant, soldier and colonist from New England, led the English conquest of Acadia in 1654, under the orders of Oliver Cromwell.

It was during this year that Sedgwick, or at least his troops, are said to have burned the Alexander estate at New Ross. The Alexanders were not French by any means, but they were still not tolerated by Cromwell, whose goal was to destroy all royalty. Cromwell, in fact, had King Charles I beheaded in 1649.

While all of this was taking place in Nova Scotia, things were moving along in New England as well.

The Plymouth Colony had begun to thrive, after a very rough start. In 1629, the Massachusetts Bay Company obtained a royal charter to plant a colony in New England, as well.

John Winthrop joined the company, pledging to sell his English estate and take his family to Massachusetts if the company government and charter were also transferred to America. The other members agreed to these terms and elected him governor on October 20, 1629.

For the remaining 19 years of his life, Winthrop lived in the New England wilderness, a father figure among the colonists.

In the annual Massachusetts elections, Winthrop was chosen governor twelve times between 1631 and 1648, and during the intervening years he sat on the Court of Assistants, also known as the Colony Council.

Winthrop settled at Boston, which quickly became the capital and chief port of Massachusetts. Boston is located only about 40 miles from Plymouth.

While on paper these were two distinct colonies, Plymouth and Boston were filled with mostly Puritan occupants who ran local government and cooperated in many ways. Those who didn't agree totally with the Puritan control of Plymouth and / or Boston often moved into areas that became Rhode Island, New Hampshire and Connecticut.

By July of 1654, Richard Bellingham, a political opponent of John Winthrop, had taken over control as governor of the Massachusetts Bay Colony.

Charles de la Tour controlled Acadia at this time, but his defenses were weak. He had outlasted his rival, Charles de Menou d'Aulnay, only to suffer financial attack by d'Aulnay's creditor, the La Rochelle merchant Emmanuel Le Borgne.

Robert Sedgwick left Boston on July 4, 1654, with 170 men in three ships and a ketch. In ten days he reached the Saint John River where he found La Tour at his fort. Three days later La Tour and 70 fighting men surrendered.

On July 31st, Sedgwick's expedition sailed to Port Royal. Sedgwick was ambushed but won the battle and took the fort. He then sailed to Pentagouet on the Penobscot River in present-day Maine, which he took on September 2nd. By early September he was back in Boston. His son-in-law, Major John Leverett, was appointed military governor of Acadia / Nova Scotia, and Sedgwick left for England, taking La Tour with him.

Oliver Cromwell welcomed Robert Sedgwick's action because the possession of Acadia provided additional bargaining power in negotiating with France.

Cromwell agreed to recognize La Tour's title to Nova Scotia under his earlier rejected grant from Sir William Alexander, which included Mirligaiche or Mirliguesche, and thereby Oak Island, but only if he would reimburse Sedgwick for the cost of the conquest, nearly £1,800.

This led La Tour to sell his rights to Thomas Temple and Col. William Crowne, who became proprietors of Nova Scotia.

Originally, there was meant to be a partnership between Sir Charles de la Tour, Thomas Temple and William Crowne. However, La Tour simply could not afford to pay off the debts he was burdened with, so he sold out to Temple and Crowne, who split Nova Scotia between them in 1657, with Temple owning the east coast, including Oak Island.

Next to the La Tours, Temple would be the second individual to specifically own Oak Island. His charter stated that the northernmost reaches of his land included Mirliguesche and, as I have shown, this area appears to have included Oak Island and all of Mahone Bay, based on the 1684 French map, and based on the original La Tour charter, which described Mirliguesche or Mirligaiche as extending beyond LaHave, fifteen leagues.

LaHave to the northeastern edge of Mahone Bay is only about 25 miles by sea. Claude de la Tour's grant extended from LaHave "following along the said coast unto Mirliguesche, near unto and beyond the port and cape of LaHave drawing forward fifteen leagues within the said lands and seas."

This could only mean northeast, along the coast.

In the English speaking world of the day, a league was three nautical miles, or 3.452 miles. Fifteen leagues times 3.452 miles equals 51.78 miles, or far beyond even Peggy's Cove, let alone Mahone Bay, if traveling by water.

From LaHave to the opposite, or northeasternmost point of Mahone Bay, approximately at Bayswater (a town located on the northeastern shore of Mahone Bay) it is only about 25 miles if traveling by water.

A modern-day map also shows it to be just over 50 miles to Bayswater, if traveling by highway. So fifteen leagues by land would still put you far past Lunenburg, and even to the far shoreline of Mahone Bay.

This appears to prove that Mirliguesche or Mirligaiche did not denote only Lunenburg, as is typically said, but also included Mahone Bay, and thereby Oak Island.

If my research and figures are correct, then Sir Thomas Temple, Knight Baronet of Nova Scotia and Governor of Nova Scotia, owned Oak Island.

Upon the restoration of the crown to Charles II, this king honored Cromwell's grant of Nova Scotia to Thomas Temple and William Crowne, and went a step further by naming Temple a Knight Baronet. Temple was a grandson of Sir Thomas Temple, 1st Baronet of Stowe, through his son John Temple. This left the family with two Baronet titles, one at Stowe, England, where the younger Temple was born, and one in Nova Scotia.

Temple then leased William Crowne's portion of Nova Scotia and was named governor for life. Unfortunately, this position only lasted until the Treaty of Breda of 1667, in which Nova Scotia was returned to France.

Temple had governed Nova Scotia for nine years, from the time he bought his rights from La Tour, in 1656, until he was ordered by the British crown to hand over his rights to the French by the Treaty of Breda.

From 1667 to 1673, Thomas Temple lived in Boston and continued to seek compensation from the king for his expenses and losses in Nova Scotia. In 1672, when a fund was being raised to build a new building for what was then Harvard College, he donated £100 out of a total of £800 raised in Boston.

Some familiar Oak Island names are associated with Harvard as well, including Roosevelt, Bowdoin, Vaughan and others.

In a way, it is odd that Charles II would grant a Knight Baronet title to Thomas Temple. Temple's surname came from an old Knights Templar headquarters in England. People from this area became known as "de Temple," or "of Temple." This was the family of Thomas Temple. This place was also where Charles I was beheaded by Cromwell. On the jury that convicted the king sat Thomas Temple's uncle, Peter Temple.

Once Charles II, the son of the beheaded king, was restored to the throne, Peter was given a sentence of life in prison, but the balance of the Temple family seems to have escaped the king's revenge, especially Thomas Temple, Knight Baronet of Nova Scotia.

Sir Thomas Temple, now of Boston, never married, but he apparently did have a mistress, a Mrs. Martin. Although he swore it was due to poverty, he spent his remaining days living at her home in England.

By the late 1630s, New England colonies (especially Massachusetts) were rapidly expanding, and Native American tribes were increasingly encroached upon. English advancements in the Connecticut River Valley led to the bloody Pequot War in 1637.

Plymouth officially condemned the harsh actions of Massachusetts against the Pequot tribe but, in 1643, still joined with that colony and Connecticut in forming the New England Confederation.

In 1691, the Plymouth Colony officially became part of the province of Massachusetts.

This brings me to a more complete story of the third subject of this chapter – Sir William Phips.

Phips was born February 2, 1651, in the Maine region of the Massachusetts Bay Colony, specifically near present-day Woolwich, Maine. He went from a sheep herder to a Boston ship captain and treasure hunter. He was the first New England native to be knighted, and the first royally appointed governor of the Province of Massachusetts Bay.

Phips was famous in his lifetime for recovering a large treasure from the sunken Spanish galleon *Concepción*, but is perhaps best remembered today for establishing the court associated with the infamous Salem Witch Trials, with which he grew unhappy and forced the court to prematurely disband after five months.

Phips has also been connected to Oak Island, and some believe he buried part of the *Concepción* treasure there. I believe the near opposite was true and that he was in Nova Scotia looking for treasure.

A man named James Philp (also written as Philip and Phelps) was the personal secretary for William Alexander. He wrote and witnessed many of the Knights Baronet of Nova Scotia documents. When William Alexander died in 1640, James Philp sold his land in Scotland and nothing is known of him from that point forward. William Phips's father was James Phips, and he shows up in Maine six years later, in 1646, with no known past record.

Phips, Philp, Philip and Phelps are shortened forms of the surname Phillips. When James Phips died, his wife married his business partner. She gave her name as Phillips, not Phips, even though her own son, William, always went by the name Phips.

It is at least possible that James Philp, secretary to William Alexander, was the same man as James Phips of Maine. Therefore, it could have been through his own father that William Phips (also at times spelled Phipps) heard of some type of treasure buried in Nova Scotia.

Spelling was just not very consistent back then. For example, in a 1628 safe passage letter written by the king for William Alexander the younger, the word ships is spelled schippis, schippes, and schips.

Even in the Freemason documents from that time, Mason is spelled Meason, along with other strange versions, plus deacon is spelled deakon, and whole is spell haille. Philp could have easily become Phips.

If so, this would explain where James Philp vanished to, where James Phips came from, why his wife gave Phillips as her surname, and how William Phips learned of a treasure in Nova Scotia.

After a visit with the king, William Phips sailed from London in 1686 to recover treasure from the *Concepción,* which sank in 1641 off the coast of Hispaniola.

He returned with a vast treasure the following year, most of which went to Christopher Monck, his financier, and to King James II, who had followed his brother, Charles II, to the throne.

King James II is said to have knighted Phips in June of 1687, although I have scoured all British knighthood records and I can find none for William Phips.

I have a theory that Phips received an honorary knighthood, and that Christopher Monck, who had by now relinquished all of his titles due to a disagreement with King James II, simply gave his unused Order of the Garter knighthood medallion to Phips as an additional reward. In any case, the medallion was dated 1671, and all indications are that it is the same one found near the foundation at New Ross.

It is known that Monck gave a very expensive gift to Phips's wife, so why not an unused knighthood medallion to Phips himself?

Somehow that medallion made its way to New Ross and I can think of, nor have heard of, any better theory.

Now known as "*Sir* William Phips," he arrived back in Boston in the summer of 1688 and was welcomed as a hero. He was celebrated in sermons and at a Harvard College commencement, and was even compared to Jason of the Argonauts fetching the Golden Fleece.

Later that same year, King James II was ousted by William of Orange, who was the son-in-law of James.

The turmoil in England, with William's accession to the throne, prompted New France's governor to take advantage of the political turmoil in New England, launching a series of "Indian raids" across the northern frontier in 1689 and early 1690. When a frontier town in Maine was overrun in early March 1690, the French were perceived as instigators and the provisional government of Massachusetts began looking for a Major General to lead an expedition against the French in Acadia.

William Phips accepted the role in late April. Leading a fleet of seven ships and over 700 men, he sailed from Boston to the Acadian capital of Port Royal. On May 9th, he summoned the French commander to surrender.

On May 23, 1690, in his own journal, William Phips wrote that he and his Nova Scotia invasion force "kept gathering plunder both by land and water, and also underground." New Ross is located only about 60 miles away from Port Royal, as the crow flies. There is a record of Phips making it as far as LaHave. If he also visited New Ross, he may have lost Monck's medallion there.

I can think of no other logical explanation, as Monck was never in Nova Scotia but Phips definitely was, and was absolutely looking for plunder "underground."

In 1692, William Phips was appointed the first royal governor of Massachusetts Bay Colony by King William. His commission specifically states that this colony would include "Acadie or Nova Scotia." Phips eventually fell out of favor with the king and was recalled to London where he died within a month of arriving, on February 18, 1695, having just barely turned 44 years of age.

*Chapter Four*

# ROOSEVELT, DELANO, BOWDOIN AND CHILDS

This book is not meant to present a chronological order of treasure hunting on Oak Island, but rather to show its specific connection to people once living near Plymouth, Massachusetts – people, in some cases, who were directly related to the families that arrived on the *Mayflower* and, in other cases, even to men who signed the **Mayflower Compact**. As a reminder of why this is important, Nova Scotia was expressly created to protect the people who came on the *Mayflower*. This is proven history, which I've outlined in the previous chapters.

It's time to get down to the actual individuals who came from the Plymouth Colony region to Oak Island over a considerable period of time, seeking a treasure whose legend may have been kept alive within these families and in the families of Knights and Freemasons.

Perhaps no other name is quite as impressive for an Oak Island treasure hunter as that of President Franklin Delano Roosevelt, who followed in his own grandfather's footsteps by showing an interest in Oak Island, and who invested with Henry L. Bowdoin in the Old Gold Salvage Company, beginning about 1909. Franklin's maternal grandfather was Warren Delano Jr., who was also an investor in an earlier Oak Island excavation.

Above is a fairly famous photo taken on Oak Island in 1909. The man in the white shoes with a pipe is Franklin Roosevelt, future President of the United States. Standing just to his left (with the bow tie) is Henry Livingston Bowdoin, who often went by the nickname Harry. The use of both Harry and Henry has caused some confusion but, as it turns out, Harry is simply a form or nickname of Henry, especially in Great Britain.

Also in the photo, may or may not be Frederick Robbins Childs, a partner to Roosevelt and Bowdoin.

These partners all descended from Puritan families who came to America *before* William Alexander's men left Nova Scotia in 1632. These Scots were at Port Royal specifically (at least on paper) to protect the Plymouth colonists from any French threat in Nova Scotia.

Roosevelt became a Freemason just two years after this picture was taken, and a Grand Master in 1934.

I did not find much information on Childs except that he descends from Benjamin Childs, a Puritan who came over in 1630, when Boston was founded about 40 miles above Plymouth. Frederick was living at Roxbury (now absorbed as part of Boston) when he became a partner. The backgrounds of Roosevelt, Delano and Bowdoin luckily are more well-known than that of Childs.

Among the many signers of the **Mayflower Compact**, important to our story, are John Howland, Richard Warren and Francis Cooke, whose nephew Phillipe de la Noye did not sign the compact or come over on the *Mayflower*, but was originally a passenger on the *Speedwell*, and made it to Plymouth the following year.

There is a direct family connection to John Howland, one of the signers of this compact, through Franklin Roosevelt's own grandmother, Mary Rebecca Aspinwell, who was a Howland descendant, and who married Isaac Roosevelt, FDR's grandfather.

Franklin's great grandfather, James Roosevelt, was married three times. While FDR descended from his first marriage, the third marriage of James was to Harriet Howland, also a descendant of John Howland.

Franklin's own father had first married a Howland woman, said to be his sixth cousin, but again Franklin was a product of his father's second marriage to Sara Ann Delano, herself a descendant of Phillipe de la Noye.

John Howland was the thirteenth of the principal men who signed the compact. In fact, his name appears directly under Richard Warren (signer number twelve), from whom FDR also descended on his maternal side.

Phillipe de la Noye, or Delano, was related to, and lived with his uncle Francis Cooke, who also came on the *Mayflower*. While Phillipe didn't sign the compact, Francis Cooke was, in fact, the seventeenth signer.

Therefore, three forefathers of FDR were known signers of the **Mayflower Compact**, and another was a very early resident of Plymouth. There may be even more signers or at least Plymouth families related to Roosevelt, if all marriages were thoroughly investigated.

Roosevelt also fits into our other two categories. He was a Grand Master of Freemasonry; and Thomas Temple, Knight Baronet of Nova Scotia (apparently a one-time owner of Oak Island), was FDR's forefather.

This last item is a considerable piece of news and, like a lot of my research, is uniquely presented only in my writings... at least so far.

Warren Delano Jr., likewise, was descended from Phillipe de la Noye, that being the original version of the Delano name. This would also then make Francis Cooke a forefather to Warren Jr.

Warren Delano Jr. and his father Warren Delano Sr. shared the first name of Warren because they both also descended from compact signer Richard Warren.

The two families of Roosevelt and Delano were on differing paths until Warren Delano Jr.'s daughter, Sara Ann, married FDR's father, James Roosevelt.

Roosevelt's link to another forefather, Sir Thomas Temple, Knight Baronet of Nova Scotia, goes back at least as far as Temple's grandfather, Sir Thomas Temple, Knight Baronet of Stowe.

The elder Thomas married Hester Sandys. Their son was Sir John Temple, who inherited the Stowe baronetcy. John's son was Thomas Temple, who added the Nova Scotia baronetcy, and who purchased Mirligaiche as part of his larger ownership of Nova Scotia lands.

Another child of John Temple was a daughter named Mary, who was wed to Robert Nelson in England. This couple had two sons, Temple Nelson and John Nelson.

John Nelson came to Boston in 1680. He was the nephew of Sir Thomas Temple, Knight Baronet of Nova Scotia and, since Thomas never married and had no recorded children, he left his entire estate to John along with his holdings in Nova Scotia, presumably including Oak Island, but certainly Mirligaiche. Nelson became very prominent in Boston and married Elizabeth Tailer, niece of Governor William Stoughton, and sister to Lieutenant Governor William Tailer, both serving the Province of Massachusetts Bay.

William Stoughton helps complete our circle of connections in a couple of ways. First, some historians say he was born in the Massachusetts Bay Colony in 1631, one year before William Alexander's Scotsmen were forced out of Nova Scotia. Second, Stoughton was chosen in 1676 to be an agent representing the colonial interests of England. Stoughton's instructions were to acquire land claims from the heirs of Sir Ferdinando Gorges and John Mason that conflicted with some Massachusetts land claims in present-day Maine. In order to do this he would have had to study the early history of these claims very closely.

These claims were secured for £1,200, incurring the wrath of Charles II, who had intended to gain them for his brother, the Duke of York and future King James II.

William Stoughton was preceded as Governor of Massachusetts Bay by Sir William Phips, under whom he also served as the head of a special tribunal for the Salem Witch Trials.

Stoughton graduated from Harvard, a college partially funded by Sir Thomas Temple, and he helped Harvard stay alive through some trying times, mostly in 1696.

For his work in protecting Harvard from possible extinction, one of the Harvard College dormitories in Harvard Yard is called Stoughton Hall. Construction of the first Stoughton Hall in 1698 was made possible by Stoughton's £1,000 gift (worth $215,000 US, today).

It could not have been lost on Franklin Roosevelt, a Harvard graduate himself, that two of his forefathers had helped keep the college alive, and that Stoughton Hall was named for a member of his own ancestry.

John Nelson's association with William Stoughton, and his marriage into the Tailer family, along with his relationship to Sir Thomas Temple, left him a very powerful and well connected man in Massachusetts Bay, and very connected to Nova Scotia as well.

In private correspondence between Thomas Temple and John Nelson, now held by Harvard University, Temple writes twice about how he: "Bought of Mon. de la Tour all his lands lying in Acadia and Nova Scotia, beginning at Mirliguesche to LaHave, etc…"

Of all his vast lands, he mentions Mirliguesche first.

John Nelson was captured by the French while on a voyage to Nova Scotia, and was imprisoned in Quebec. It was common for local privateers to receive commissions in Boston but to be considered pirates by the other nations of the world, especially the French and Spanish, who were the other superpowers at the time.

While in prison, Nelson learned about secret French plans for attacks against the Massachusetts colonies. He discreetly informed the Massachusetts authorities of this information from his prison cell. For this act, Nelson was punished by being transported across the Atlantic Ocean to the legendary Bastille prison in France.

In 1702, after ten years of imprisonment, his uncle, Sir Purbeck Temple, obtained his release. Purbeck was one of three brothers of Thomas Temple.

Nelson immediately returned home to Nelson's Island (now Long Island, MA) as a local hero. This is where the families of Franklin Roosevelt and Henry Bowdoin begin to intersect.

But first, to finish Roosevelt's connection to Sir Thomas Temple:

•Nelson's daughter, Rebecca, married Henry Lloyd;

•This couple had a daughter, Margaret, who married William Henry Smith;

•William and Margaret had a daughter, Rebecca, who married John Aspinwall;

•From this marriage came John Aspinwall Jr., who married Susan Howland of the *Mayflower* family;

•Their daughter, Mary, was wed to Isaac Roosevelt, grandfather to Franklin Roosevelt on the paternal side.

This puts Sir Thomas Temple, Knight Baronet of Nova Scotia, Governor of Nova Scotia, and likely owner of Oak Island, as a proven forefather to Franklin Delano Roosevelt, a lifelong fan of, and searcher for, a buried treasure on Oak Island.

It is said that Roosevelt was following up on an old family legend, and this is often explained as being due to his maternal grandfather, Warren Delano Jr., being an investor in another group which explored Oak Island in the mid 1800s. What if both men were following up on a family legend kept alive through their *Mayflower/* Knights Baronet/Freemason families?

Could the legend of a treasure be kept alive within a family for nine or ten generations?

I am living proof that it could.

You see, my own family has a legend, which has a fair amount of proof to support it, of a treasure brought from Great Britain to the Carolinas, which was eventually given to Sam Houston to pay Texas war debts. The will that bequeathed the treasure is still on record in England. The stories of the treasure are still alive in many branches of the family. The land deed for 10,000 acres of Texas, granted in return for our family's treasure, is also still on record in a courthouse in Texas.

This treasure story began ten generations ago for my family, and is still talked about today. Old family letters and court filed documents concerning it still exist.

So why, in families so powerful and rich, couldn't an Oak Island legend remain active for an equal period of time, especially for a treasure that was still missing?

Without my own family's experience, and without all of the hidden history I have uncovered, I might be tempted to think of this as a conspiracy, or at least a fantastical theory. But, as they say, the proof is in the pudding, and we have a lot more to digest, including how Henry Bowdoin was related to his partner Franklin Roosevelt.

As stated, Sir Thomas Temple left his estate, including his Nova Scotia property, to his nephew, John Nelson.

You may also remember that it was Purbeck Temple who affected Nelson's release from the Bastille prison. Purbeck was a brother of Thomas Temple and he had a son that he named Thomas, as well.

The younger Thomas Temple had a son named Robert, who had a son named John Temple. This John Temple made a bid to acquire the titles of Knight Baronet of Stowe and Knight Baronet of Nova Scotia.

He was the first British consul-general to the United States and the only British diplomat to have been born in what later became the United States. He was sometimes known as (but not universally acknowledged to be) Sir John Temple, 8th Baronet of Stowe, and in some histories he was considered a Knight Baronet of Nova Scotia.

Sir John Temple was born in Boston in 1731. John's father was Robert Temple and his mother was Mehitabel, daughter of John Nelson mentioned above. John Temple served as lieutenant governor of New Hampshire. He married Elizabeth, the daughter of James Bowdoin, Governor of Massachusetts, and this is the link of the Bowdoin family to Franklin Roosevelt.

Elizabeth, the daughter of John Temple and Elizabeth Bowdoin, married Thomas Winthrop.

Thomas descended from John Winthrop, one of the leading figures in the founding of the Massachusetts Bay Colony, the second major settlement in New England following the Plymouth Colony. John Winthrop led the first large wave of colonizers from England in 1630, and served as governor for 12 of the colony's first 20 years. He was governor for two years before William Alexander's men were forced out of Nova Scotia.

Thomas Winthrop's wife was the daughter of John Temple who inherited Thomas Temple's Knight Baronet title. If ever there was a time for a legend of something buried on Oak Island to be passed down within a family, this would have been one of those times.

From Thomas Winthrop and Elizabeth Temple came a daughter, Sarah, who married George Sullivan, son of James Sullivan, 7th Governor of Massachusetts. George and Sarah had a son, George R. J. Sullivan. This younger George married Frances Hamilton, a descendant of Alexander Hamilton, the famous America statesman.

George R.J. Sullivan and Frances Hamilton had a son who oddly took the surname Bowdoin. Thus, George Sullivan III was known as George Sullivan Bowdoin.

George Sullivan Bowdoin and his wife, Edith Grinnell, had a son, Temple Bowdoin, who was an associate of J.P. Morgan & Company, and was elected a member of the New York Stock Exchange in 1909, the exact same year that just a few steps away, at 46 Broadway, Henry Bowdoin was forming the Old Gold Salvage Company.

Henry Livingston Bowdoin had his business office at 46 Broadway, NYC, a building just a short walk from Wall Street. Built in 1900, the building is still in use today as a health clinic and other medical offices.

Henry claimed to have found $2,000 in treasure based on information he received from a few African Americans down south. This supposedly set him on a course to search for treasure and to make money selling stock in the search. This may have been a story, true or not, that he used to convince others that he was a viable treasure hunter. Henry also dealt in mining stocks out west under the name Boston-Arizona Mining Company as of 1901, but claimed there was no money in it.

Throughout his life, Bowdoin patented a number of mechanical designs and machinery, mostly diving equipment, and was an engineer and stockbroker.

Henry L. Bowdoin moved into his Broadway office in 1903. From there he ran ads across the country for investors who wanted to make a big return on their investment fast. There was little information on how.

In 1909, he created the Old Gold Salvage Company and announced he was financing the whole project himself. Shortly thereafter, he started selling stock up to at least $250,000 (which would equal over $7,000,000 in today's US dollars). Henry Bowdoin thought big!

This is when his collateral relative, Franklin Roosevelt, joined the team. Franklin had spent many summers as a youth sailing in the Bay of Fundy, and even searching for treasure on that side of Nova Scotia. It seems he was ready to go on a new adventure to Oak Island.

The exact genealogy of Henry Bowdoin has not been proven yet. There are two web sites that vary widely on who his parents could be, but neither offers proof.

One thing is very obvious. Henry's middle name was Livingston and, as we've seen, using the maiden name of the mother for the middle name of a child was very common back then. It just so happens that Temple Bowdoin's father, George Sullivan Bowdoin, was a business partner of Carroll Livingston, who had a brother named Henry Livingston, and so it is almost certain that Henry Livingston Bowdoin comes out of this family legacy, in some fashion. Perhaps a daughter of Henry Livingston Carroll married a son of George Sullivan Bowdoin, this couple having a son Henry.

With Henry Livingston Bowdoin working only a short distance from Temple Bowdoin in New York City (both as stockbrokers), and Temple's father being a partner to Carroll Livingston (brother of Henry Livingston), the evidence is stacking up in favor of Henry Livingston Bowdoin being a close relative of Temple Bowdoin.

He would therefore be a collateral relative of Franklin Roosevelt, of Sir Thomas Temple, and of others who could be "in the know" about Oak Island.

It is true that Henry Bowdoin wrote an article in a 1911 issue of *Collier's Magazine* claiming that there was nothing to be found on Oak Island. There are reasons to believe this was a ploy to fool other treasure hunters.

First, Bowdoin asked Fred Blair, the exclusive lessee of Oak Island, to renew the sublease for his search attempt. If he was so sure there was nothing there, why do this?

Second, Henry Bowdoin kept his Old Gold Salvage Company in business until 1912, a year after his article denouncing the possibility of an Oak Island treasure, and three years after leaving Oak Island. Again, why?

Third, Henry Bowdoin's investor and distant relative, Franklin Roosevelt (a very intelligent man), continued to believe in an Oak Island treasure for the rest of his life.

I wonder if, once Henry couldn't get his lease renewed by Fred Blair, he thought he'd throw everyone off the scent by writing the *Collier's* article. Or maybe he wrote it to get his investors off his back.

The Old Gold Salvage Company may have struck out on Oak Island, but they left behind some very interesting family genealogies showing how a legend of treasure buried there could easily be handed down through many family lines for many generations. The study of their families also offered up some interesting facts about Harvard, first known as Harvard College, and later as Harvard University.

Quoting from an ardent historian of Harvard graduate biographies, Alicia Crane Williams:

> *These biographies demonstrate how rarified the college experience was in the seventeenth century. In the first volume (1642–1658) class size averaged 5.4, ranging from zero in the classes of 1644 and 1648 (and one in the class of 1652) to a maximum of ten in 1651. The men who attended the college came from the elite of the elite, sons and grandsons of the men who controlled the religious, political and financial world of the colony.*

I've already pointed out how Sir Thomas Temple and William Stoughton were benefactors of Harvard, and how their collateral relative Franklin Delano Roosevelt graduated from Harvard. In fact, eight presidents of the United States have graduated from Harvard, along with eight signers of the Declaration of Independence, or as Williams states, "the elite of the elite."

Of course Harvard had a head start, being the first college founded in America (1636).

Paschal Nelson, a son of John Nelson, graduated from Harvard in 1721. William Stoughton graduated from there in 1750. His own father, Israel Stoughton, was one of the original incorporators of Harvard. There are also Temples, Bowdoins, Vaughans and other recognizable alumni names, some as collateral relatives of Roosevelt.

The second ever graduate of Harvard, one George Downing, is an interesting figure. The famous Downing Street in London is named for him. After graduation in 1642, Downing returned to Great Britain where George Monck made him a member of Parliament for Scotland.

Downing was actually a spy and a spy master, both in Scotland, and later in Europe. Though he worked for Monck and Cromwell, when Charles II was restored, he switched sides. He actually arrested some of the men who had beheaded Charles I, and was a master of politics and intrigue. In the end, Downing was considered by some as the epitome of a traitor until Benedict Arnold came along to fill that role. It is possible that he was a spy for Monck and Cromwell while in North America, as he rubbed elbows with the "elite of the elite."

*Chapter Five*
# CHAPPELL, CRANDALL AND ROGERS

One of the more recognizable names among Oak Island treasure hunters is that of Chappell. It is not a coincidence that this name sounds like the word chapel, as it is said to derive from a person who lived at a chapel in France, who was known as de la Chapel or Chappell. The first notice of the Chappell name, for our purposes, is a man named John Thomas Chappell.

When the *Speedwell* finally limped into port, it can be imagined that few wanted anything do to with her after her ill-fated attempt to sail to America along with the *Mayflower*. The *Speedwell* was already an old ship by then, built in 1577. An identically sized ship to the *Speedwell*, also named the *Speedwell*, had already been to North America. Some say it was the same ship; others disagree. Regardless, the *Speedwell* had already participated in the 1588 battle against the Spanish Armada, and had been on a military expedition to the Azores in 1596.

English separatists had moved to Leiden, Holland, with one of their leaders, Captain Thomas Blossom, who bought the *Speedwell* in Holland. The *Speedwell* left the Netherlands on July 22, 1620, and was later sailed under command of Captain Reynolds to Southampton, England, to meet her sister ship, the *Mayflower*.

As a merchant investor in the colony, Captain Blossom was also responsible for the purchase of the *Mayflower*. Since Blossom was in this, at least to some degree, for the money, he had no reason to hang onto the *Speedwell* and it was sold to John Thomas Chappell.

Under the new ownership of Captain Chappell, the *Speedwell* sailed again on May 28, 1635, from Southampton, England, finally arriving in Virginia. The ship then returned to England where it was refitted and sold again.

According to some Chappell family historians and genealogists, George Chappell was the son of John Thomas Chappell, captain of the ship *Speedwell*.

George came to the Plymouth Colony in 1635 on a ship called the *Christian*. His brother Thomas came to America on a ship called the *America*, which landed at the Virginia Colony in the same year. His father's ship, the *Speedwell*, landed in America, also at Virginia, and also in 1635, with John Thomas Chappell on board.

And so it appears that these Chappell men left for America about the exact same time, but on three separate ships, which makes sense if you wanted to make sure at least one member of the family made it there alive.

George Chappell's family settled at New London and then Lebanon, Connecticut, about 23 miles apart, and only 100 miles or so from Plymouth. Of special interest is that George was said to be born at Barnstable, England.

Barnstable, Massachusetts, is only 30 or so miles from Plymouth, MA, and was named for Barnstable, England, George Chappell's birthplace.

What once was Barnstable County, UK, is now known as Barnstaple, and a town within the county is also called Barnstaple. Lying just outside of Barnstable/Barnstaple County in England, is the port of Plymouth, England, where Ferdinando Gorges served as governor, and where the *Mayflower* left from English shores on her way to the New World.

However, Plymouth, England, is not the last place you'd see as you sailed out into the ocean. Two towns with familiar names are located further out on a slim point of land jutting into the Atlantic. These are the towns of Falmouth, England, and Truro, England.

The second organized group of financiers and workers assembled to search the Money Pit was called the Truro Company, because most of its members came from Truro, Nova Scotia. This Truro got its name in 1759 from New England settlers moving there and naming the town in memory of one of the last sights their ancestors saw as they sailed away from England on the *Mayflower*, and/ or perhaps one of the last sights they saw as they left Massachusetts.

The name of Truro, England, goes back to Richard de Lucy de Trivereu, who had a castle in that area about A.D. 1140. There have been a few explanations for the meaning of Trivereu (the original name for Truro). It seems it could have meant the three rivers, the three roads, or three river roads.

Regardless, the name of the town gradually changed from Trivereu to Truro, and that name eventually made its way to Nova Scotia.

However, the name "Truro" made a stop in New England, just a short distance from Plymouth, MA.

Truro, Massachusetts, is located along a similar neck of land jutting out into the ocean as that of Truro, UK.

This area was named about 1709 by the Puritans from Plymouth, but that was not their first stop at this place.

The story I told in chapter one of this book, about Thomas Howland, Richard Warren and others landing a small sailing craft on the shoreline as they searched for the best spot for the *Mayflower* passengers to come ashore, took place at what later became Truro, MA.

Less than a year later, some of these same men, and their immigrant families, are believed to have celebrated a productive harvest with the Natives Americans they called "Indians." This was the catalyst for the annual Thanksgiving holiday celebration in the United States.

Truro, Nova Scotia, is not alone in owing its name to Englanders and New Englanders. There is the town of Falmouth near Plymouth, England, another Falmouth near Plymouth, Massachusetts, a Falmouth in Maine, and a Falmouth in Nova Scotia – the same town name being used over and over by English immigrants. This name literally means "mouth of the Fal (or fallow) River."

Well, the same held true for Barnstable County, MA, being named for Barnstable (now Barnstaple) County in England, and both counties are just next to Plymouth in each country. Even Boston, Massachusetts, was named for Boston, England, from where the Puritans of England first sailed over to Holland for religious freedom before coming to America.

George Chappell was born in Barnstable, UK, in 1615, and came to America in 1635, settling at the Plymouth Colony as a Puritan. George's son Caleb was the father of two sons, Joshua and Jabez Chappell.

Joshua Chappell's son, Joshua Jr., married Bathsheba Brewster, whose ancestor was William Brewster, the third man to sign the **Mayflower Compact**, connecting the Oak Island Chappell family to another man who signed this document. Jabez, the other son of George, was in the line of the Oak Island Chappells. From John Thomas Chappell to these Chappells, the line would be:

- *John Thomas, owner of the Speedwell;*
- *George, resident of the Plymouth Colony;*
- *Caleb;*
- *Jabez;*
- *Eli;*
- *Charles, who settled in New Brunswick;*
- *James;*
- *Lucius;*
- *Renwick and William;*
- *William's son, Melbourne.*

William Chappell, who was a lumberman and mill operator, gave an extensive report of his work on Oak Island. Perhaps the most interesting bit of information is that, at about 171 feet, his drillers hit iron. Their bit was dulled after about an hour of drilling, only dropping one quarter inch. The drill was then re-sharpened and tempered for drilling into iron. After another two hours of drilling only one more quarter inch was achieved.

Filings on the drill bit were subjected to a magnet and proved to be iron. This, and the recovery of a cement-like substance, were sworn to, before a Notary Public.

William Chappell worked on Oak Island in 1895 as part of the Oak Island Treasure Company. Although this was one hundred years after the Money Pit was allegedly found, Chappell made some amazing discoveries. It is even said that he found traces of gold on a drill bit but attempted to keep his discovery a secret.

William was joined by his brother, Renwick Reid Chappell, who later wrote a private report, only recently made available, outlining many of the finds and the work done on Oak Island. He called his document *Read, Think and Reason.* In it he reproduced sworn statements from many people, including descriptions of when a small piece of parchment was found, when metal was found on the drilling auger, and other critical points in the history of the Oak Island dig.

By the way, this parchment still exists and is in the hands of the current Oak Island team.

Melbourne Russell Chappell (1887-1981), a member of the Chappell family who came to Nova Scotia from New England, was the son of William Chappell, one of four brothers who operated the successful firm of Chappell Brothers, Builders & Contractors.

M. R., as he was often known, was born at Chappell's Mill, Cumberland County, NS, in 1887. This county is located just above Truro. He was a draftsman in the office of his father's construction firm located in Sydney, Cape Breton, NS (later known as Chappells Ltd.).

M.R. Chappell is best known for carrying on a forty-year search for buried treasure on Oak Island, which he purchased in the 1930s, and continued to explore until his death in 1981.

Both William and Renwick Chappell married women whose maiden names were Crandall. Flora Crandall married William Chappell. Lydia Crandall married Renwick Chappell.

The jumping off point of the causeway, in order to cross over to Oak Island, is called Crandall's Point and was named for the family of these women.

With the help of John Makidon, whose mother was Mary Alice Crandall, I think I have made another important discovery about Oak Island, based, once again, on family connections. John sent me a link to a Crandall family history book from 1881, which included several interesting connections, including the Crandall link to the Plymouth Colony.

I was always a fan of the hidden significance of family connections within my own family, and I have learned to be this way about Oak Island history too. During my research for my book *Oak Island Endgame* I found that many early landowners and searchers on Oak Island were related in one way or another to the Knights Baronet settlement attempt of Nova Scotia ending in 1632, and also to known Freemason families from 1634 onward.

To my surprise, these two groups of people eventually expanded to include families living in or near the Plymouth Colony. Learning this information led me to the writing of this book, *Oak Island And The Mayflower*.

A good share of the Crandall family in North America considers John Crandall (known as "Elder John") as their progenitor. John was a resident of the Plymouth Colony around 1634, although his family moved on to Rhode Island, and some eventually to New Brunswick and Nova Scotia.

We now have the Crandall family connection to the Plymouth Colony, and to the very last point of land on the mainland that one touches before heading over to Oak Island – Crandall's Point.

Both the Vaughan and Crandall families came to Oak Island, having earlier lived in Rhode Island, which was part of the Plymouth Colony until Rhode Island split off in 1636. So when we see Crandalls or Vaughans born in Rhode Island we can know they were still part of this diaspora of *Mayflower* passengers and the Plymouth Colony, whether they came on a later ship or not.

The Crandall line widened considerably from the time of Elder John Crandall of the Plymouth Colony. One branch was led by Wilbur Crandall who married Mary Vaughan. Their son, Peter Crandall, of Chester, NS, married another Vaughan woman, Rebecca Vaughan.

The little church on the road heading to Crandall's Point and to the Oak Island causeway was probably the one established by David Crandall or his father, Wilbur, who married a sister of Anthony Vaughan Jr.

I'll have more on the Vaughan family in my next chapter, but these many intermarriages are interesting, and it has to be remembered that most people "married within walking distance" back in those days.

The Crandall family lived at Mahone Bay and also at Digby, NS, which is very near to where William Alexander's original Port Royal settlement was. David Crandall was the minister at Mahone Bay, as well as at Digby and a few other places in Nova Scotia. These two locations (Mahone Bay and Digby) are of interest because of their connection to Sir William Alexander and to Oak Island. So, at this point, we have an early family of the Plymouth Colony named Crandall now in Nova Scotia at both Mahone Bay and in the Annapolis Valley, and we have them marrying into the Vaughan family (with Anthony Vaughan Jr. being one of the first to dig at the Money Pit site) and into the Chappell family.

Whether this is another branch or not, Ebenezer and Henry Crandall also came to Nova Scotia in 1874. They signed some legal agreements to build a ship, which eventually went nowhere, involving them in a lawsuit.

Their company was called Crandall Brothers and eventually the Crandall Brothers Construction Company. This branch of the family was involved at Halifax, Nova Scotia, not far from Oak Island.

James Thomas Crandall lived in New Brunswick, as did many others from the original Elder John Crandall line. Among his children were daughters Flora and Lydia. As we earlier mentioned, Flora married William Chappell and Lydia married Renwick Chappell. The Chappells had also lived in New Brunswick for awhile before moving into Nova Scotia. This could loosely tie even the Crandall family to a signer of the **Mayflower Compact** through these marriages to Chappell men.

By now, we have at least five famous Oak Island treasure hunters directly associated with the Plymouth Colony and, more significantly, with the **Mayflower Compact** – William Chappell, Renwick Chappell, M.R. Chappell, Franklin Roosevelt and Warren Delano Jr.

But there may be a sixth!

In a document prepared on July 6, 1818, by William Nelson and David W. Crandall, various names, relative to their respective lots on Oak Island, were recorded for the Nova Scotian crown lands office.

As of 1778, seventeen years before the Money Pit was found, Jeremiah Rogers is shown owning lot 27.

I've discovered that Oak Island landowner Jeremiah Rogers was almost certainly a descendant or close relative of Thomas Rogers, one of the men aboard the *Mayflower*, and one of the signers of the **Mayflower Compact**.

Rogers, the Oak Island landowner, was a privateer at the same time as Samuel Rogers. Jeremiah and Samuel are very common names in the Rogers family of the Massachusetts Colony.

On April 1, 1620, Thomas Rogers sold his house in Holland in preparation for his voyage on the *Mayflower*. He came on the *Mayflower* with his eldest son Joseph, leaving behind his younger son John, his daughters Elizabeth and Margaret, and his wife Alice.

Thomas Rogers, nineteenth signer of the **Mayflower Compact,** died the first winter at Plymouth, leaving behind his 18-year old son Joseph. His wife and children, who were left in Holland, are found in a 1622 tax poll as "poor people" and "without means."

Elizabeth and Margaret apparently came to New England later, but where they lived or whom they married remains unknown. However, the son, John, came to Plymouth about 1630.

Jeremiah Rogers, of Oak Island, descended from four ancestors in a row named John, and his great, great grandfather John was in Plymouth at least by 1632, when his son, the second John Rogers, was born. Since there were very few people in Plymouth at the time, it is almost certain that John Rogers of Plymouth from 1630 is the same John Rogers of Plymouth from 1632, forefather to our Jeremiah Rogers.

This then makes Jeremiah Rogers our sixth person associated with Oak Island who is also associated with a signer of the **Mayflower Compact**.

Samuel Rogers is on two lists along with privateer James Anderson, another Oak Island landowner. One is a record of Revolutionary war pensions. Another is a list of eight privateers that came out of the "merchant class" of Boston. In a separate record Samuel is recorded as having been on the crew of a privateer near Cape d'Or on the Bay of Fundy, when their ship was destroyed and he and others escaped into the forest of Nova Scotia.

As for Jeremiah, I found many additional records.

In one, he is listed as one of two captains who were monitoring the coast between Connecticut and Long Island, where apparently trade was prohibited or at least strongly regulated. Their intent was to prevent unauthorized commerce and traffic between Connecticut and Long Island.

In some cases, goods were allowed to be brought into Connecticut but it was illegal to trade or sell anything outside the state without permission. A more aggressive goal was "to land on Long Island and there take all British property."

In this 1781 record Jeremiah was being chastised for having "unjustly and cruelly plundered many of the friendly inhabitants there, brought off their effects, and have caused them to be libelled and condemned in course of law."

Another record is of Jeremiah during the French and Indian War - 1756 to 1763.

This record states "The majority of the cruises starting from Halifax were directed against the French in southern waters, and the commissions authorizing them generally named six months as the period during which they might be lawfully prosecuted. Captain Sylvanus Cobb, Jeremiah Rogers and others engaged in cruising along the shores of this Province, in the Bay of Fundy, and against the French at Chignecto, Minas Basin and the River St. John."

This puts Jeremiah Rogers near Oak Island as early as 1756 -1763, but actually he was near the island even sooner.

Captain Jeremiah Rogers was with Governor Edward Cornwallis when Halifax was founded by the British in 1749. Government dispatches mention him as early as January of 1751 and, on May 29, 1753, he was to be found transporting soldiers to Mahone Bay to prepare the new township of Lunenburg very near to Oak Island.

Then, on June 7th of that same year, he began transporting 1,453 German settlers there as well. This would mark the first time in recorded history that such a large group of people lived anywhere near Oak Island. A French census taken in 1688 recorded ten Europeans and eleven Mi'kmaq settled in Mirliquesche. However, by 1745, there were only eight settlers recorded as living in the region.

Captain Rogers was also responsible for transporting troops, mail and supplies to forts and outposts all around Nova Scotia. He was present at the deportation of the Acadians in 1755, and at the capture of the fortress of Louisburg in 1758. During his time as a sea captain for the province, he was granted lands in most of the townships around Nova Scotia. He had command of four ships during his career with the government. The first ship, the *Ulysses*, sank in 1758 while trying to sail up the St. John River.

(Credit goes to Doug Crowell for digging up a lot of the information in this section.)

On October 21, 1758, it was reported that Jeremiah Rogers lost the *Ulysses* while attempting to navigate some treacherous waterfalls and rapids. He was then given command of a brand new ship named the *Montague*.

This ship also sank (this time in the Canard River) after bringing settlers from New England into the newly created townships of Cornwallis and Horton in 1760. Captain Rogers continued in service to the province until at least 1766, during which time he captained the sloop *Amherst*, and another ship named *Nova Scotia Packet*.

On Doug Crowell's website, he reproduces a few notices on Rogers. Here's one:

> *1766, Jan. 9*
> *The schooner Nova Scotia Packet, Captain Jeremiah Rogers, outbound for Boston. Source: Atlantic Canada Newspaper Survey Pages 20 – 21*

There are indications Rogers died in 1795, the same year the Money Pit depression was found.

So there we have it – six big names connected to Oak Island and also to signers of the **Mayflower Compact** – Franklin Roosevelt, Warren Delano Jr., Jeremiah Rogers and three Chappell men, William, Renwick and M.R.

One thing many Oak Island searchers had in common was their membership in Freemasonry. We know that at least two of these men connected to the signing of the **Mayflower Compact** were also Freemasons, and we have photographic proof, with M.R. Chappell at left, and FDR on the right, both wearing their Masonic aprons.

*Chapter Six*

# McGinnis, Smith, Vaughan and MacLean

Beyond sounding somewhat like a trustworthy law firm, the surnames McGinnis, Vaughan and Smith are perhaps the most common names mentioned in regard to the Money Pit on Oak Island. I've thrown in Hector MacLean here (the uncle of John Smith) because he may be one of the most important landowners on Oak Island in support of my theory.

Daniel McGinnis is typically said to be the first person to notice a depression on Oak Island (in 1795) which seemed like there might be more to it than what first met his eye. He then engaged his friends John Smith and Anthony Vaughan to begin a dig that, little did they know, would continue for the next 225 years.

John Smith purchased the Money Pit lot that same year from a merchant in Lunenburg who may have initially acquired it for the lumber it contained, or for land speculation purposes.

The original legend states that these three people were all teenage boys when they discovered the pit. From their own reminiscing, as recorded by others during the early years of the Money Pit dig, they claimed to have found several rotting tree stumps and some new growth of trees in and around the depression.

One modern Oak Island author recently pointed out that this would indicate the pit could be no older than the 17th century, simply based on the description of the stumps and newer trees.

Apparently, this conclusion has also been drawn by a few arborists hired by the Oak Island team. This pleases me to no end, especially when coupled with carbon dating and artifact dating that also points to the 17th century. This matches the history I've uncovered, leading to my theory and my current Plymouth Colony research – all pointing to William Alexander and the year 1632.

Add in five other authors who hinted at Alexander being involved, and a couple more who point to the 17th century, and my theory is certainly earning its #6 spot in the top 25 – maybe even someday the #1 position.

The families of Anthony Vaughan, John Smith and Daniel McGinnis came to Oak Island from the area surrounding the Plymouth Colony, particularly Boston.

We know this, in part, because of the book *Western Shore, Gold River, Martin's Point,* written by Willa Kaiser, which states that Daniel McGinnis (with a variety of spellings) came to Nova Scotia, along with the Smith and McMullin families from New England.

Proof can be found in several other sources.

Based on his own research, Doug Crowell verified that the Smiths did come from Boston where John's father, Duncan Smith, was a blacksmith. Therefore, we can be reasonably sure that John Smith's family came to Oak Island from Boston, along with the families of Daniel McGinnis and Neil McMullin. But there's more!

Neil McMullin married Margaret Smith when Duncan died. Neil must have been a good stepfather, as John Smith named his first son Neil McMullin Smith. The arrival from Boston is further verified in a biography of Neil McMullin Smith, first born son of John Smith, which says the Smiths came to Nova Scotia from Boston, where Duncan Smith married Margaret MacLean.

There is some pre-Revolution writing concerning the future wife of a John MacLean of Milton, a town located ten miles from Boston and thirty miles from Plymouth.

John was an early and major donor to Harvard and a Freemason in Boston. The words read: "The tradition is that she went to the house of her kindred, Jeremiah Smith. From the intimate relations ever existing between the Smith and MacLean families, it is highly probable that she made the family of Mr. Smith her home."

While we can't be sure that these people are relatives of Hector MacLean or his sister, Mrs. Duncan (Margaret) Smith, the expression of closeness between the Boston area families is of interest. Obviously, Margaret MacLean had to meet and marry Duncan Smith somewhere, and we know that he was a blacksmith in Boston.

There is also a biography of Murdoch Campbell Smith, son of Neil McMullin Smith, stating that he was the "son of Neil... and Elizabeth Bezanson Smith, and was born in Kings County, NS, Feb. 10, 1856." The biography further states that his ancestors were among the earliest settlers of Nova Scotia, his father's people leaving Scotland about 1755 or 1760, and coming to New York where they lived for a short time.

According to Murdoch, they then drifted to Boston, where two children were born. They left Scotland during stormy times for America and did not find this country a bed of roses, for soon after the outbreak of the Revolution they are found living in Halifax. The bio states: "Somewhat later his father took a government grant of land situated on Oak Island, in Chester Basin."

We know it was actually Murdoch's grandfather, John Smith, who took advantage of the grant on Oak Island, probably a grant given to Duncan Smith.

Immigration from Scotland to New York, to Boston, and to Nova Scotia, matches what Doug has found.

The history of Milton, Massachusetts, states that it was first settled by Puritans in the 1630s, and that many settlers arrived during the 1650s, fleeing the aftermath of Oliver Cromwell's fall from power and the English Civil War. The Smith family history says that they left Scotland about 1755 or 1760.

Murdoch's bio further states: "His mother's people settled with the German colony in Lunenburg County, soon after the settlement of Halifax."

A Bezanson genealogy site tells us: "The Bezanson family was originally from Montebeliard, France." Jean Jacques Bezanson (b. 1754, d. 1806) was the son of Jean George Bezanson and his wife Jeanne, who immigrated on May 16, 1752, to St. George's Island, Halifax, Nova Scotia, aboard the *Speedwell* (of all ships). When Jean died in 1806, his will stated: "I Give and Bequeath unto my well beloved son, Joseph, all the land or lands I have possessed of on Oak Island."

Jean Jacques Bezanson was also known as John James Bezanson and he is shown owning lot 32 as of 1807.

With all this detailed information, it can be safely accepted that John Smith's father, Duncan, came from Boston along with the families of McMullin, Smith, and likely MacLean. It can also be assumed that they were Loyalists who left New England for the safety of British held Nova Scotia.

This certainly seems to be the case for the elusive Hector MacLean, uncle to John Smith.

A Hector MacLean is given as the 7th Knight Baronet of Nova Scotia in the MacLean line. According to the website *Clan MacLean History Project*, Hector MacLean, 7th Knight Baronet, joined the British 84th Regiment of Foot (Royal Highland Emigrants), headquartered at Fort Edward, Nova Scotia, located only about 40 miles from Chester and from Oak Island.

It appears this second iteration of the 84th Regiment was partly formed by Hector's predecessor, Sir Allan MacLean, 6th Knight Baronet, out of four groups of Highland volunteers who had settled in Canada at the peace of 1763, after the French and Indian War. This regiment served in New England, the Carolinas, and widely throughout Canada, but especially in Nova Scotia. Two places of interest where they saw action were at Lunenburg and in Mahone Bay, which puts this Hector MacLean within a few minutes of Oak Island.

Some in the MacLean family feel this Hector MacLean is the same man as the 1784 landowner on Oak Island, which seems more than believable.

The *London Gazette* newspaper records that a Hector MacLean was promoted to Lieutenant from the 1st Battalion of the 84th Regiment of Foot to the 100th Regiment of Foot on the 8th of May in 1784 – the 84th Regiment of Foot being disbanded in 1783 after the American Revolutionary War.

To review, Hector MacLean, of Oak Island, is recorded in 1784, the same year that possibly the same Hector MacLean, Knight Baronet, is recorded 40 miles away, as part of the 100th Regiment, serving at Lunenburg and Mahone Bay, within minutes of Oak Island. If this was, in fact, Sir Hector MacLean, 7th Baronet, this puts an actual Knight Baronet of Nova Scotia on Oak Island as one of the earliest landowners!

Where it gets a little sticky is that Hector MacLean of Oak Island represented Hants County in the Nova Scotia House of Assembly from 1793 to 1799, while Sir Hector MacLean, 7th Baronet, is said to have gone into a quiet retirement. Both of these statements could be true, if Assemblyman Hector MacLean simply and quietly stepped back from his titles in England.

Granted, there have been many Hector MacLeans in history, but how many of them have been on Oak Island or within a few minutes of Oak Island in the exact same year? Seems too close to be a coincidence.

One thing I've discovered in my years of historical research is that a lot of people hedged their bets during severe times of trouble, cautiously choosing one path without burning their bridges with an alternative path.

This could be the case for Hector MacLean.

It can at least be accepted that Duncan Smith, John's father, and Hector MacLean, John's uncle, came to Oak Island from nearby Boston, a city founded shortly after Plymouth, and located just forty miles away. If they were actually from Milton, MA, they would have lived just thirty miles away from Plymouth.

I've already made considerable mention in my earlier books of the MacLean family, about how there is a record of Lachlan MacLean, Knight Templar, followed years later by Lachlan MacLean, Knight Baronet of Nova Scotia (forefather to our Hector MacLean), followed many years later by James MacLean, Second Grand Master of the Freemasons of France.

The MacLean family was very strong in Scotland with their main castle, Duart Castle, on the Isle of Mull. This castle is where escaping Knights Templar are said to have taken refuge in 1313.

If Hector MacLean of Oak Island was indeed the 7th Knight Baronet of Nova Scotia from the MacLean line, it is highly unlikely that he would be unaware of the goings on of William Alexander's settlement in Nova Scotia, including the 1632 departure.

With James MacLean of Scotland as leader of the French Freemasons, even more inside information would have been available to the family.

And with the propensity of both Freemasons and Scottish families to keep exhaustive records, especially of family connections (but also of military records), any information about a buried treasure on Oak Island could certainly be passed down in their family histories.

There is further evidence that Hector MacLean of Oak Island was, in fact, Hector MacLean, 7th Knight Baronet of Nova Scotia, in the form of his predecessor, Allan MacLean, the man who established the 84th Regiment, as the 6th Knight Baronet of Nova Scotia.

I don't mean to belabor this point, but the significance of having a Knight Baronet as an actual landowner on Oak Island is tremendous. We already know that Sir Thomas Temple, who almost certainly owned Oak Island as part of his Mirligaiche grant, was also titled a Knight Baronet of Nova Scotia.

Official information available on Sir Allan MacLean, 6th Knight Baronet, states: "He was born in 1710, in Torloisk, to Donald MacLean, 3rd Laird of Brolas. He became the Clan Maclean chief when Sir Hector MacLean, 5th Baronet, his third cousin, died without an heir in 1750. During the American Revolutionary War he was promoted to the rank of colonel, and MacLean and his men were instrumental in the defeat of **Benedict Arnold** at Quebec."

Official information available on Allan MacLean of the 84th Regiment states: "During the defense of Quebec he was appointed second-in-command by Governor Guy Carleton, often sleeping in his uniform in Quebec City while the city was threatened by a rebel army under **Benedict Arnold** which had appeared mid-November."

The same event + the same **Benedict Arnold** = the same Allan MacLean.

The MacLean Baronetcy of Morvern was created in the Baronetage of Nova Scotia on September 3, 1631.

Due to some lines dying out with no heir, the title devolved onto the MacLeans of Torloisk, where Sir Allan was born. He eventually received the honor but, having no children himself, the title of Knight Baronet fell on his cousin Hector MacLean of the 84th and 100th Regiments, and almost certainly of Oak Island.

Once again the possibility of a legend of treasure on Oak Island being kept alive through the MacLean family is obvious: a family from near Plymouth and Boston, a family important to Freemasonry, and a family filled with Knights Baronet of Nova Scotia. These are the groups that I contend held information about something buried on or in the vicinity of Oak Island.

The land of Hector MacLean may have been part of the Shoreham Grant of 1759, which allowed cheap or free land grants after the expulsion of the Acadians. The British wanted to repopulate vacated lands, and offered land grants to colonists from New England.

In 1761, led by founders Timothy Houghton and Rev. John Seacombe, New England Planters were granted land in an area called Shoreham, which included the Chester area and Oak Island.

A large part of Oak Island was originally owned by the Monro, Lynch, Seacombe and Young families, who had been granted the island in 1759. Richard and Johanna Seacombe settled in Boston, Massachusetts, in 1680. In fact, these were all New England families and, it appears, the first to come directly from there to Oak Island. Remember, John Monro, also spelled Munro, was related to William Alexander through his son-in-law.

As for the Young family, they had long been close to the English kings, James I and Charles I, both involved in the creation of the Knights Baronet of Nova Scotia. The one lot the Lagina team is not yet able to access on Oak Island still belongs to Robert Young.

John Monro actually helps prove my Hector MacLean theory.

Monro had openly declared his loyalty to the Crown even before the outset of the American Revolutionary War. He was the first Loyalist to offer his services to Colonel Allan MacLean of Torloisk, 6th Knight Baronet of Nova Scotia, and his newly formed 84th Regiment of Foot (Royal Highland Emigrants).

John eventually acquired 10,000 acres of land and senior offices in Upper Canada. In 1788 he was made Sheriff and a member of the land board for the Lunenburg District. Though there is variation in the spelling of his surname between Monro and Munro, this is obviously the same Monro family of Oak Island, since John was Sheriff of the Lunenburg District as of 1788, and was recorded as owner of Lot 12 on Oak Island as of 1781.

I will show, in a later chapter, how he was related to Sir William Alexander's son-in-law, Robert Monro.

This brings us to Daniel McGinnis.

There are two sources in Scotland for the McInnis or McGinnis name. Innis (with no Mc) was a northeastern Scotland name, referring to an island or the land between two rivers. Sir Robert Innis of Innis was actually the first clan chieftain to sign up as a Knight Baronet after the original partners of William Alexander.

However, King James had promised my forefather, Donald MacDonald MacUisdean, the premier position because the MacDonalds were so powerful at the time. When it came down to it, Donald took second place to Robert Gordon, an intelligence agent for the king.

The Gordon line remained in the premier position until 1908, when it died out. This moved the line of Sir Ian MacDonald MacUisdean up to the premier position, where it remains today.

Even though I had shared emails a few times with Sir Ian before I sent a small piece of information to the Oak Island team back in 2016 about the Knights Baronet of Nova Scotia, I had no idea what these knights were really all about. I've certainly learned a lot about how they settled as the first English-speaking people in Nova Scotia, how they were the catalyst for the establishment of Freemasonry, and how they might even be responsible for the Oak Island mystery.

It is less likely that the Daniel McGinnis family came from this Innis Knight Baronet family than it would be that he came from the McGinnis family of northwestern Scotland, particularly the northern Highlands and the western islands of Scotland, including the Isle of Skye, from where many Nova Scotian can trace their lineage.

This second source for the McGinnis name would be a family which was part of a group of vassal clans to Clan Donald. Among these families was also the surname McMaster and, at times, MacLean – all very common names in Nova Scotia. In this case, McGinnis was a form, or later variant, of MacAngus.

MacMaster was actually the name of a specific chief of the McGinnis clan, eventually becoming its own clan, similar to the MacUisdean/McQuiston family being named for a chief of Clan Donald, Uisdean MacDonald.

It was a rule of Highland culture that, if a chief was of significant stature or importance within a family, a new clan name could be created for his family line.

McMaster and McQuiston are examples of this, as is Clan Donald itself, being named after a grandson of the great Celtic/Viking hero Somerled. McGinnis was also created this way for a chieftain named Angus. McAngus became McGinnis. These branch clans were often called "septs," and when you research particularly prominent clans you will often see sept names listed as well.

Other examples are Wilson, Jamieson and Georgeson which often emanated from Clan Gunn.

Some names even came from locations where the clan lived. For instance, the Calhoun family of Loch Lomond was originally the Kirkpatrick family "of Calhoun." Eventually, the Kirkpatrick part was dropped for the surname Calhoun.

We also have discovered that George Sullivan III took the surname Bowdoin, so I guess this tradition carried on even into modern times. This shows why it is important to look at the broadest history of any family before making assumptions.

The Daniel McGinnis/McGinnes/McInnis/McKinnis family could have come from either group, but would still be linked, one way or the other, to the Knights Baronet families and Sir William Alexander.

One thing we know for sure is that the McGinnis family came to Oak Island from Boston, and they would have had some past link to William Alexander, either through the Innis baronetcy or through their common link to Clan Donald by way of the McGinnis clan.

History tends to support the McGinnis family of the islands and Highlands as the source for this name.

It seems to be proven by now that it was Donald McGinnis, the father of Daniel McGinnis, who actually received or purchased a grant of land on Oak Island.

The Shoreham Grant brought many New Englanders to Nova Scotia, especially around Chester and Oak Island. Other New Englanders arrived during or after the American Revolution, around Truro and Onslow.

New England families were coming up to Nova Scotia for many reasons, from wars to simply fishing or trade. In 1753, Oak Island was given to two New York fish merchants, Richard Smith and John Gifford, along with a couple other islands. By 1762, Oak Island was surveyed and divided into 32 equal lots. This is the only island in Mahone Bay where this has happened. Could it be just a coincidence that 32 lots were created on an island that may have had a treasure buried on it in 1632?

As stated, the earliest actual Oak Island lot owners were the Monro, Lynch, Seacombe and Young families.

The Lagina team has, by now, come into control of 78% of the island. Fred Nolan, a long time Oak Island landowner and searcher, left his lots to his son Tom, who has allowed at least some exploration, particularly metal detecting, to take place on his property, as well.

Daniel McGinnis, son of Donald McGinnis, is nearly always credited with making the first discovery of the Money Pit depression. He then brought in two friends to help dig it up – John Smith and Anthony Vaughan, Jr.

I just can't help but wonder if McGinnis, Smith and Vaughan were purposely looking for a treasure in the vicinity, based on family legends passed down for generations that spoke of William Alexander's venture into Nova Scotia. This seems as though it could be true for most of the families that I am featuring in this book.

Our third Money Pit digger, Anthony Vaughan Jr., was the son of Anthony Vaughan, who also received a grant of land on Oak Island, and whose family not only traces back to New England, but also to a very close friend of Sir William Alexander.

William Alexander was closely associated with a man named William Vaughan, who had a similar, speculative colony in Newfoundland. A 1910 *Americana* magazine story of the Knights Baronet states: "As a direct result of the publicity campaign conducted by William Alexander, Robert Gordon and Dr. William Vaughan, and the creation of the Knights Baronet, the enterprise (Nova Scotia) received a new impetus."

Alexander and Vaughan were close friends, sharing an interest in Rosicrucianism. Vaughan's brother, Henry, wrote an enigmatic line, shortly after the beheading of King Charles I, that reads: "Thus is the solemn temple sunk again, into a pillar, and concealed from men." One definition for the word pillar is "a shaft," and a shaft is synonymous with a tunnel, passage, or pit.

Using a few Vaughan family genealogies I was able to discover the complete connection of William Vaughan, friend of William Alexander, to Anthony Vaughan Jr. I have, for a long time now, suspected that Anthony Vaughan Jr. of Money Pit fame was related to William Vaughan, friend to Sir William Alexander, the Scottish owner of Nova Scotia, and the man who actually named the province in 1621.

I believe I now have the proof.

The furthest back I could go with the Vaughan name was March 24, 1599, to a pedigree created in Wales. From these records I learned that Sir Roger Vaughan of Bredwwardyn, Wales, had several sons who also became knights. One of these was Watking Vaughan, father to Sir Walter Vaughan, and the grandfather of Sir William Vaughan, the friend of Sir William Alexander.

This line would then be:

*Sir Roger Vaughan;*
*Sir Watking Vaughan;*
*Sir Walter Vaughan;*
*Sir William Vaughan.*

Another one of Roger's sons was Sir Thomas Vaughan, brother to Watking. From Thomas on down, I was also able to find the line of Anthony Vaughan Jr. based on the Wales pedigree, but also based on later Vaughan family records, and on records from Doug Crowell's *Blockhouse Investigations*, from the *Atlantic Canada Genealogy Project* records, and from Chester, Nova Scotia, land and family genealogy records.

This would then be the line for Anthony Vaughan Jr.:

*Sir Roger Vaughan; born in Wales;*
*Sir Thomas Vaughan, born in Wales;*
*David Vaughan, born in Wales;*
*John Vaughan, born in Wales;*
*John Vaughan, born 1628, in Rhode Island;*
*David Vaughan, born 1646, in Newport, Rhode Island;*
*John Vaughan, born 1671, in Newport, Rhode Island;*
*David Vaughan, born 1704, in Newport, Rhode Island;*
*Anthony Vaughan Sr., born April 6, 1751, in Scituate,*
*Providence, Rhode Island;*
*Anthony Vaughan Jr., born Aug 25, 1782 in West*
*Chester, Lunenburg, Nova Scotia.*

The Vaughan family of Rhode Island was very widespread in the 1600s, and at least one Vaughan man married a Howland women, which would mean we'd have another possible connection to a signer of the **Mayflower Compact** and Oak Island.

The records get too murky to pursue, but there is little doubt that all of these Rhode Island Vaughans were related as they came to Plymouth from Wales, then moved into Rhode Island where the dissenters of the Puritan ways had set up their own community.

Some of these men were recorded with the alternative spellings of Vaughn or Vahan.

However, as far back as the Wales records, and the records of William Alexander's friend, William Vaughan, the original and most common spelling has been Vaughan.

Anthony Vaughan Jr. was one of the Money Pit's original searchers. His sister Mary wed Wilbur Crandall, whose family had also come to the Mahone Bay area from Rhode Island, but had originally landed in America at the Plymouth Colony.

David Vaughan, grandfather of Anthony Jr., moved from Rhode Island to Dutchess County, New York, about 1758. He is listed in the February 3, 1761, tax list for Beekman's Precinct. He died in 1761 at Beekman, and his will was probated in Albany, NY, on October 30, 1761.

After his death, several of his children emigrated to Nova Scotia as New England Planters, including Anthony Vaughan Sr. and his brother Daniel, both early landowners on Oak Island.

There are records that say the Vaughan brothers also came to Nova Scotia with the McGinnis and Smith families.

Daniel and Anthony Sr. built a saw and grist mill near each other on a stream known as "Vaughan's Stream," on Chester's Western Shore.

According to Doug Crowell: "Among the very first Oak Island lot owners was Anthony Vaughan Sr. He acquired Lot Nos. 15 and 17 in 1765 and then Lot No. 14 in 1781 – the same year that Anthony's brother Daniel bought Lot No. 13. The Vaughn (or Vaughan) family history says that Anthony Sr. and Daniel moved from Duchess County, NY, to settle in the Chester area in the 1760s. The two brothers had equal shares in a saw mill somewhere in the local area. Possibly, they bought the island lots to have access to the timber for their mill."

Beekman is a town in Dutchess County, New York, United States, so both of these records agree on the location of David Vaughan before his family moved to Nova Scotia. It is said that Anthony Sr. and his brother Daniel had another brother, John, already living at Chester when they arrived. A record in Chester shows that John Vaughan owned land in 1764.

So it can be assumed that the Vaughan brothers arrived at Chester in the early 1760s, likely after their father passed away in 1761. There were many intermarriages of the Vaughan family with other significant Oak Island names, as was the case with so many of these Oak Island families.

Since the Vaughans had a link back to William Alexander and to the Plymouth Colony, they check off two of my criteria for Oak Island landowners and treasure hunters - the Plymouth connection and the Knights Baronet connection, or at least a connection to the creator of the Knights Baronet of Nova Scotia.

William Vaughan may even have played a role in the creation of the Freemasons, since it was he who introduced William Alexander to Rosicrucianism.

Entire books are written on the genealogy of a single family that are much larger than this book, and so it is likely that many more pieces of information exist for all of these families that I have not yet seen, but that could further solidify the connections of them to the Plymouth Colony, and to William Alexander's attempt to settle Nova Scotia. This leaves open the possibility that at least some of them knew about a treasure on Oak Island.

*Chapter Seven*

# RAMSAY, STRACHAN AND MONRO

One family name connected to the Plymouth Colony that plays a major role in my other two categories of Oak Island searchers or landowners (Freemasons and Knights Baronet) is the name Ramsay.

The first we hear of this surname in regard to our story is John Ramsay, 1st Earl of Holderness, known as Sir John Ramsay between 1600 and 1606, and as the Viscount of Haddington between 1606 and 1621.

John was listed as one of the signers of the charter for Plymouth of 1620, the charter Sir Francis Bacon was a leading figure in obtaining. Also on that list were William Alexander and Ferdinando Gorges.

John had also become Lord Ramsay of Melrose in 1609. John's wife died December 6, 1618, and none of their children survived to adulthood. Possibly due to his grief, he resigned the title of Lord Ramsay of Melrose in favor of his cousin, Sir George Ramsay. Other records say George was actually his brother.

George had the title changed from Lord Ramsay of Melrose to Lord Ramsay of Dalhousie. It was a later George Ramsay, Lord Dalhousie, who left his position as Grand Master of the Scottish Freemasons, and founded Dalhousie University just an hour from Oak Island.

Four Ramsay men became Knights Baronet of Nova Scotia, and many have led the Scottish Freemasons.

So here we have a family who financially supported the Plymouth Colony, who signed on as Knights Baronet, and who has been a significant name in Freemasonry since its very beginnings, checking off all three of our Oak Island landowner/searcher boxes.

Dalhousie University is located roughly an hour from Oak Island in Halifax, Nova Scotia. There are a few campuses located elsewhere, and it is highly-respected.

Through the years, this citadel of learning has been involved with Oak Island in a number of ways, from the translation of the 90 foot stone (by a Dalhousie professor), to a fiction novel with Oak Island at its heart (written by a Dalhousie professor), to providing a meeting room for the Oak Island Association, and even to rumors of a large room containing shelves of Oak Island artifacts.

The cornerstone of the university reveals that Lord Dalhousie had recently been the Grand Master of the Scottish Freemasons. Among the men who attended the laying of the cornerstone were the Grand Master of all Nova Scotia Freemasons, along with the Grand Wardens, Officers, and Brethren of all of the Halifax Lodges.

I don't think you could tie Freemasonry any closer to Dalhousie University's beginnings than this list of men who were present at the cornerstone laying event.

Lord Dalhousie was George Ramsay. He was related to the world's fifth Freemason, David Ramsay, who was closely related to Alexander Strachan, thief of the treasure I think might be buried on Oak Island.

George's father, also named George, had been Grand Master of the Freemasons as well, and his son, James Broun-Ramsay, followed in this tradition. Four Ramsay men led Scottish Freemasonry nearly in a row.

George would also be related to the current Grand Master of Scottish Freemasonry, William Ramsay McGhee, whose mother was Janet Ramsay, and who often goes by the nickname of "Ramsay."

The Ramsays were connected to Al Strachan through intermarriage, and two of Sir William Alexander's ship captains were William and George Ramsay.

David Ramsay, closely related to Al Strachan, not only served as a personal aid to King Charles, but also became the world's fifth non-operative, accepted Mason, on August 25, 1637. Just the year before, Lodge #1 of Edinburgh used the term Freemason for the first time, in this case as "Frie Mesones," written December 27, 1636.

Ramsay was sponsored by the Alexander brothers and Al Strachan. The actual record reads: "This 25th day of August 1637, David Ramsay one of his Majesty's special servants is admitted a fellow and brother of craft, and thereto we have subscribed or set to our marks. Alexander (William Alexander, Jr.), Anthony Alexander, Alexander Strachan, John Mylln, John Watt."

Through e-mail exchanges with Kel Hancock, Grand Historian of the Grand Lodges of Freemasonry in Nova Scotia, I was led to the book *History of The Lodge of Edinburgh #1*, by David Murray Lyon, Grand Steward of the Grand Lodge of Scotland (1873), where these first Freemason records were found.

This book was actually dedicated to Fox-Maule Ramsay, Lord Dalhousie, who was the nephew of George Ramsay, Lord Dalhousie, the man who had established Dalhousie University.

The dedication page reads: "To The Right Honorable The Earl of Dalhousie, K.T. G.C.B., Past Grand Master Mason of Scotland, Past Deputy Grand Master of the United Grand Lodge of England, etc."

Beyond these Ramsay Grand Masters in Scotland, there were many other Ramsay men serving in other positions within the Freemasons.

It is easy to see that the name Ramsay is and has been very significant to Scottish Freemasonry.

The Lord Dalhousie for whom this book was dedicated was named Fox-Maule Ramsay, and he must have been especially influential in Freemasonry having at some point led both the Scottish and English Freemasons. The book, or at least part of it, was written at Dalhousie Cottage in Scotland, as indicated by the signature of its author, David Murray Lyon, a Grand Steward of the Lodge of Scotland and Senior Grand Warden of Ayrshire, Scotland.

It was also in this book that I found the story of the treasure stolen by Alexander Strachan and photographic copies of the actual initiation records from 1634 for William Alexander Jr. and Anthony Alexander, and also for Alexander Strachan.

In addition, it was in this book that I found the record for David Ramsay, when he became the world's fifth non-operative, accepted Mason.

The connections to my theory and to Oak Island of both the Ramsay family and Dalhousie University are very extensive. For instance, I found an original Knight Baronet charter held by Dalhousie, and only transcribed once in a book written in 1934.

The fact that Dalhousie University even has this 17th century document is pretty remarkable, especially when you consider it contains the original signatures of many of the men involved in my Oak Island theory including Sir William Alexander and Sir Alexander Strachan.

Sir Gilbert Ramsay of Balmaine was one of the earliest men, mostly clan chieftains, to pay the expensive fee to become a Knight Baronet in 1625. In all, four Ramsay men became Knights Baronet of Nova Scotia.

After the loss of the Scots settlement at Port Royal in 1632 (my target year for the Oak Island mystery to begin), the Alexander brothers entered as non-operative Masons along with David Ramsay.

By 1818, a member of this same Ramsay family, after serving as Grand Master of the Scottish Freemasons, was establishing Dalhousie University just an hour away from Oak Island.

We have a proven historic connection of a Ramsay investor in the Plymouth Company to four Ramsay Knights Baronet of Nova Scotia, to the sizable Ramsay leadership of Freemasonry, and to Dalhousie University, built about an hour from Oak Island by a Ramsay.

What more could we ask for in making a direct connection between these historic events? And the evidence seems to point to Oak Island as the endgame.

There is a small amount of evidence that Al Strachan may have signed as a witness to one of Sir William Alexander's official New England documents, although he only played this minor role in New England history that we know of. But not so with Oak Island.

As a review, Al Strachan stole a large treasure in Scotland in 1622-23 that has never been accounted for. Instead of being convicted, he was given a complete pardon and became a partner with William Alexander, even witnessing a land charter for Mirligaiche, granted to Claude de la Tour by William Alexander. All in this paragraph is provable through historical documents.

Strachan even received his own grant of 16,000 acres of Nova Scotia land and, as a Knight Baronet of Nova Scotia, he was above the law and answerable only to William Alexander.

The story gets more interesting when we learn that a man from this same Strachan family owned land on Oak Island, and not just any land, but the lots that make up Nolan's Cross, a mysterious and significant Oak Island landmark. John Strachan owned these lots as of 1841. He owned them when the Truro Company began its explorations, with Anthony Vaughan Jr. and John Smith as advisors, and a host of New Englanders at their side. He was also a Freemason in nearby Halifax.

At this point we have a relative of one of the signers of the Plymouth Company petition (Sir John Ramsay), and a descendant of one of the main partners of William Alexander (Al Strachan) both being Freemasons, and both involved somehow in the history of Oak Island.

All we need now is a relative of William Alexander linked to Oak Island. And we have one!

I previously showed an actual record from 1794 which lists John Monro sandwiched between two familiar Oak Island names – Samuel Ball and Donald McGinnis.

But who was John Monro, and why have we not heard much about him?

That's exactly what I wondered when I found this little gem on the website belonging to Doug Crowell and Kelly Hancock.

The Monro saga begins with John Munro, 11th Baron of Foulis, and 14th Chief of Clan Munro.

John had two sons of interest to our story.

The first son, William, was the ancestor of Hector Munro, Knight Baronet of Nova Scotia under Sir William Alexander, and also of Hector's nephew, Robert Monro, who married Jean Alexander, the eldest daughter of Sir William Alexander.

William's daughter, Jean, was first married to Hugh Montgomery, and they actually named their estate in Ireland "Mount Alexander." After Montgomery's death, Jean remarried to Robert Monro, of the same family as John Monro, one of the first owners of property on Oak Island.

Robert appears to be one who changed the spelling from Munro to Monro, as his father used Munro. However, it is possible that the name was simply spelled differently by clerks as they were writing it down in official records. This has happened to many if not most families coming to America, including mine.

The second son of note, Hugh Munro, was given the lands of Coul, and was known as Hugh Munro, 1st Baron of Coul. Eight generations down from Hugh we find Captain John Munro, who came to Canada. His son was John Monro of Oak Island.

The apple never fell far from the tree for these Scottish families until immigration to North America began.

As an example, Captain John Munro was born in the county of Ross and Cromarty, Scotland. Foulis Castle is also situated in Ross and Cromarty. Ross and Cromarty were two smaller shires that were combined into one county called Ross and Cromarty. This single Scottish county was home to all of these men named Munro or Monro, just as Aberdeen was home to all the Strachan men involved in this story.

These records absolutely put a collateral relative of Sir William Alexander on Oak Island as one of the early landowners, sandwiched between Donald McGinnis and Samuel Ball on the landowners list from 1794.

This record would indicate the possibility that John Monro, relative of Sir William Alexander's son-in-law, was living on Oak Island just one year before the Money Pit was discovered, and possibly during the same year that it was discovered – 1795. What's more, John Strachan ended up owning one of John Monro's Oak Island lots!

Oak Island author D'Arcy O'Conner wrote that two of the earliest original landowners on Oak Island were men named Munro and Young. This record was from 1759.

Other records show John Monro as a lot owner by 1781, which is a long ways off from 1759.

Regardless of the year that he got there, or how his surname was spelled, John Monro was definitely a landowner on Oak Island, and at a significant point in its history.

I knew little of this when I wrote my previous books, but looking at these records now, it is absolutely amazing that later relatives of William Alexander and Al Strachan would choose to live on an island that their forefathers had included in a land charter from 1630 and (at least according to my theory) were ultimately responsible for something being buried there.

We do, however, have a pretty good idea of how John Monro of Oak Island got there. He is believed to be the first Loyalist to offer his services to Colonel Allan MacLean of Torloisk, the 6th Knight Baronet in the MacLean line, and his newly formed 84th Regiment of Foot (Royal Highland Emigrants).

Monro accompanied MacLean (in disguise) for two hundred miles through the hostile province of New York "at great risk to his own life," and was instrumental in secretly enlisting many of his tenants and neighbors, many of whom were disbanded soldiers of the British and Highland Regiments, in the new Royal Highland Emigrants, before he was arrested and thrown into jail.

In 1776, Monro was sentenced to hang, but the following year he managed to escape across the border to Canada. There is the possibility that the elder John is from the 1759 record, and the son John is from the 1781 record. Since both were named John, this would explain the long Monro stint as owners of Oak Island.

The records of these Plymouth families, Knights Baronet families, and Freemason families are nearly overwhelming when it comes to Oak Island. I have just a few more surnames to cover, which I will lump into one final chapter specifically on this subject.

It's true that there are many descendants of the people who arrived on the *Mayflower*, plenty of descendants of the Knights Baronet, and plenty of descendants of Freemasons to choose from. But the likelihood that the majority, if not virtually all early landowners and prominent early searchers on Oak Island, would come from one, two, and sometimes three of these groups certainly seems beyond coincidence, especially when the vast majority seem to be intent on finding a specific treasure there, which I believe at least some of them heard about through family legends.

It is hard to explain this phenomenon any other way, especially in the face of the history that we know took place based on the many documents I have uncovered.

Who knew Sir Francis Bacon had anything to do with the Plymouth Colony? How many people knew that Nova Scotia came about because of the people on the *Mayflower*? Who knew that Franklin Roosevelt was related to three of those hardy souls?

One revelation after another has made it into my "inbox" over the last five years. I couldn't ignore these, even though it took me awhile to realize their implication that most, if not all, of these families had heard of a missing treasure buried somewhere in or around Oak Island, NS, and then came looking for it.

*Chapter Eight*

# A HOST OF NEW ENGLANDERS

I stated in the last chapter that the Truro Company was surrounded by a host of New Englanders. This seems to be the case for many of the earliest searches on Oak Island including the Onslow Company.

I will combine the balance of my New England/Oak Island family research into this one chapter, including those men involved in these and other searches.

But first I have to take care of a few more early Oak Island landowners. One such person is Thomas Embree, who is said to have served as a Loyalist and part of the dreaded Banastre Tarleton Raiders during the American Revolution - a cavalry unit that gave no quarter. His family came to Plymouth, MA, very early on.

Anthony Vaughan sold lot 4 to Thomas Embree in 1804. The Embree family moved to Plymouth in the mid 1600s, and were not part of the *Mayflower* group, but married into it. Thomas Embree also descended maternally from John Howland, the same man that FDR descended from. We could likely add a seventh, eighth, ninth or tenth Oak Islander to the list of descendants of **Mayflower Compact** signers if we included Embree, Vaughan, Crandall and Bowdoin.

But the connection has already been clearly made.

Two early Oak Island landowners definitely tied to the Knights Baronet were Alexander Wallace and Martin Marshall, as explained in my *Oak Island Endgame* book. It is likely these men also came to Nova Scotia from New England as British Loyalists.

We begin with records of a Thomas Marshall, freeman of Boston 1634-1635, and an assignment of Indian lands to Samuel Marshall, Windsor, Connecticut, in 1663.

We next find Elijah Marshall involved, once again, with Benedict Arnold's attack on Quebec in 1775. Together with another man from Connecticut, Elijah was among the first men to mount the defending walls.

Elijah Marshall, 2nd Company, 2nd Regiment, was taken prisoner on December 31, 1775. Nearly the full complement of men called for from the Connecticut regiments for the expedition were captured.

Though I don't have the details yet, it would be interesting to witness the divided loyalties of Oak Island landowner Martin Marshall, a son or relative of Elijah Marshall, attacker of Quebec, as concerns Oak Island landowner Hector MacLean, who was among the defenders of Quebec, while part of the 84th Regiment.

It is well-known that there was a mix of Loyalists and American Patriot sympathizers in Nova Scotia. Many New Englanders who had moved there after the French and Indian War supported the rebels in the lower colonies. There were people from the same or similar family backgrounds, sometimes even related, who took opposite sides in the Revolution, very much like the English and American "civil wars."

While I could not yet make the exact connection, it is very likely that Martin Marshall descended from Elijah, since other Oak Islanders were also connected to the Benedict Arnold attack on Quebec.

It is interesting that one of the names that appears on the original Knight Baronet charter, held by Dalhousie University, is that of John Marshall. This document was signed by Al Strachan, William Alexander, Alexander's secretary James Philp, and William Keith, son of the man that Strachan robbed.

It is also the case that the title of Marischal of Scotland, held by the man Strachan plundered, became a surname in Scotland in the form of Marshall.

As for the family of Alexander Wallace, Oak Island landowner, we know there were two Knights Baronet of Nova Scotia from this family. Hugh Wallace of Castle Craigie, Ayrshire, Scotland, became a Knight Baronet in 1638. He resigned in 1659, probably because of the Cromwell movement. Hugh's title was revived by his descendant Thomas Wallace in 1670.

Thomas Wallace may have felt or known that his family descended from the great Scottish hero, William Wallace, immortalized in the *Braveheart* movie, because he had a son he named William Wallace IV.

Though a Knight Baronet of Nova Scotia, Sir Thomas Wallace moved to North Carolina, to a Scots community there. He died about 1750, and just about that same time William Wallace IV, was born. Coincidently or not, the Wallace family lived at Onslow, North Carolina, similar in name to Onslow, Nova Scotia.

Again, I could not make the exact connection of the family of Sir Thomas Wallace, Knight Baronet of Nova Scotia, living in Onslow, North Carolina, to Alexander Wallace, landowner on Oak Island.

Onslow, Nova Scotia, on the other hand, is located directly across the river from Truro. The first organized group to follow up on excavating the Money Pit was called the Onslow Company. I am sure the information exists somewhere to find Wallace's reason for being in Nova Scotia, and it is likely that he was part of the Loyalist forces, perhaps even the 84th Regiment that made their way to Nova Scotia from the Carolinas.

It is interesting to note that a contemporary of Hugh Wallace, Knight Baronet, was one James Wallace, who served as a captain under General Robert Monro, Sir William Alexander's son-in-law, when he occupied Huntly Castle of the Clan Gordon in 1640. This castle was home to Sir William's partner and, at the time, premier Knight Baronet of Nova Scotia, Robert Gordon.

The research necessary to connect the many names listed in this book has been mammoth, and all older records are subject to some misinterpretations and/or mistakes. However, for the most part, I have not printed any known mistakes or wild guesses, and I try to qualify areas where I do not have definitive proof.

There is a historical narrative, usually built around wars, but also around family migrations, that lies in the background of all of these families, whether it be at Plymouth, Massachusetts, or at Truro, Onslow or Oak Island, Nova Scotia.

These connections and historic time lines show that this story is one continuous tableau of human struggle in escaping troubles in the Old World, of dangerous travel to the New World, and of interesting exploration and mobility, once there – a mobility not so readily available back home. The on again/off again interaction between Massachusetts and Nova Scotia is explained very well in a review written by Gordon E. Kershaw of a book titled *Nova Scotia's Massachusetts: A Study of Massachusetts–Nova Scotia Relations, 1630–1784*, by George A. Rawlyk.

From this book review we learn:

*This book fills the gap between older, conventional histories of the two British colonies by analyzing their sporadic relationship from earliest settlement until the end of the American Revolution. In the words of the author, the work "is primarily concerned with describing and attempting to account for, first, the continuing economic hammerlock Massachusetts had during most of the period from 1763 to 1784 over the neighboring colony, and second, the various military thrusts sent from New England to the region to the northeast."*

*Professor Rawlyk emphasizes that this was not a relationship between equals. Clearly, Massachusetts was bound to dominate Nova Scotia, and it did, but only at intervals. The interest of Nova Scotia's powerful neighbor stemmed from economic considerations and the need to limit French expansionism. Probably these two factors account for the intermittent nature of Massachusetts involvement in the affairs of Nova Scotia.*

Her people were stirred to action only when their access to the cod fisheries was curtailed, when their peacetime (and often wartime) trade with Nova Scotia was in danger, and when France extended her garrisons and pushed southward into Maine.

Thus the attitude of Massachusetts towards Nova Scotia was ambivalent: on the one hand, fearful lest the enemy there become too powerful and, on the other, reluctant to forfeit its substantial economic investments, which depended upon amenable, if not neutral, Acadian inhabitants.

This situation continued, with variations, even after French Nova Scotia fell completely under British control in 1763.

Professor Rawlyk describes several peaks of interest in Massachusetts relationship with Nova Scotia.

The successful Phips attack on Port Royal in 1690 and the Pepperrell-Warren expedition of 1745 against Louisbourg mark two of these.

Each, however, was followed by a period of apathy coupled with antagonism toward the British, who the New Englanders believed had robbed them of credit for their great exploits.

Although they dutifully assisted in the second capture of Louisbourg, in 1759, Massachusetts residents had by then lost interest in Nova Scotia.

For this reason, Rawlyk concludes, they consigned the Nova Scotians to isolation during the political crises of the 1760s, labelling them backward and beyond redemption.

*When revolution came, Massachusetts lifted not a finger to aid a grass-roots movement for independence plotted by Yankees in Nova Scotia.*

Some have taken issue with this assessment, but it at least provides an over-arching outline to the larger story of Massachusetts/Nova Scotia interaction.

The first crew to attack the Money Pit, after the original three diggers gave up the battle, was the Onslow Company. An ardent Oak Island researcher, Scott Clarke, has done a fair amount of connecting various Oak Island families to each other. Clarke tells us:

> *Early newspaper accounts and later books all mention the same four men as being members of this group. They are Colonel Robert Archibald, Captain David Archibald, Sheriff Thomas Harris and Simeon Lynds. In a later company prospectus we learn of a fifth member of this company, Mr. William Blair Jr.*
>
> *What people usually don't know is that all five of these men were fairly closely related to each other. Robert Archibald, who was the eldest of the group, is reported to have been the leader of the Onslow Company. David Archibald was Robert's son.*
>
> *William Blair Jr. was Robert's brother-in-law, as Robert had married William's sister Hannah Blair. Another Blair sister, Rebecca Blair was married to Thomas Lynds and they were the parents of Simeon Lynds, who is credited with forming the Onslow Company. Lastly, Thomas Harris was married to Jennet Savage, the daughter of Robert Archibald's sister Margaret.*

What I can add to Scott Clarke's remarkable research is that the Archibald, Blair and Lynds families all came up from New England. Sheriff Thomas Harris came to Nova Scotia from Pennsylvania.

David Archibald was Robert's son. Robert's father was also named David and he came to New Hampshire from Londonderry, Ireland, in 1757, and moved to Nova Scotia in 1762. The elder David was the first in the Grant of the Township. He was a Justice of the Peace and represented Truro Township in Parliament.

The Blair family descended from Captain William Samuel Blair, born in Rutland, Massachusetts. Rutland is located about 80 miles from Plymouth as the crow flies, and only about 60 miles from Lebanon, where the Chappells lived before going to Nova Scotia.

In fact, Captain Blair owned many plots of land throughout Massachusetts and Connecticut and, at a time when there just weren't that many people in this area yet, it is possible that the Blair and Chappell families knew each other earlier than normally thought.

Captain Blair went to Nova Scotia in 1745. He was not a ship's captain. He was a captain in the forces that took Louisburg from the French. He later returned to Nova Scotia in 1759, along with nineteen other men, to settle at Truro and Onslow, two names associated with companies that conducted the first two organized treasure hunts on Oak Island.

From Captain William Blair came both William Jr., of the Onslow Company, and the legendary Frederick Blair, one of the most long lasting of Oak Island searchers.

Captain William S. Blair died at Onslow in 1791. His family line is as follows:

*Captain William Samuel Blair;*
*William Jr., of the Onslow Company;*
*Robert, whose daughter Mary wed William Lynds;*
*James, who wed Phoebe Lynds, sister to William Lynds;*
*William, father of Fred Blair;*
*Frederick Blair, who spent many years on Oak Island.*

Simeon Lynds of the Onslow Company, who first dug the Money Pit to 90 feet, was the son of Thomas Lynds and Rebecca Blair. Rebecca was the daughter of Captain William Blair. This means that even Simeon Lynds had a connection back to New England through his mother.

But he didn't need it anyway, because he descended from Thomas Lynde who migrated to New England during the Puritan Great Migration (1620-1640). Thomas settled at Malden, MA, just 45 miles from Plymouth. Since the exact date of Thomas Lynde's arrival in America isn't known, he could possibly have been part of the group that petitioned King James to give Nova Scotia to William Alexander. In any case, New England was well represented within the Onslow Company.

As for the Truro Company, we see the same pattern of New Englanders leading the charge. This new team leased land from the Smith family, while John Smith and Anthony Vaughan Jr. provided guidance, even though they were both in their seventies. Truro drillers allegedly found several links of gold clinging to their auger drill.

The list of Truro Company principals given by Oak Island historian Paul Troutman includes:

*Dr. Simeon Lynds - Shareholder;*
*James Pitblado - Foreman;*
*John Gammell - Shareholder;*
*Robert Creelman - Manager;*
*Adams Archibald Tupper – Foreman;*
*Jotham McCully – Manager and Drilling Engineer*

Scott Clarke adds this info:

*The Truro Company was led by Robert Archibald's cousin, Charles Dickson Archibald, who was an experienced miner and manager of the Acadian Iron Works. Another Archibald cousin who joined this company and had a long association with Oak Island was Adams Archibald Tupper.*

*Adams was named after his uncle, Sir Adams George Archibald, who became one of Canada's Fathers of Confederation. John Gammell was another investor and member of the Truro Company and he was Adams A. Tupper's uncle. A younger brother of Simeon Lynds by the name of Dr. David Barnes Lynds also became a member of this company. David also married into the Blair family.*

One man who is not listed in either report of the Truro Company is Warren Delano Jr., and yet he has been mentioned two or three times on the *Curse of Oak Island*, as well as on websites and in books, as a Truro Company investor.

One author points out that the Oak Island Association, which was based on the original Truro Company, enlisted help in securing funding for the treasure hunt through a silent partner Warren Delano, Jr., who was an accomplished mariner, trader, business organizer, and grandfather to Franklin Delano Roosevelt.

This may be where the confusion has been all along.

The Oak Island Association again included Adams Archibald Tupper, but also Isaac Blair, the grandson of Onslow Company member William Blair Jr., and Robert Creelman who was the great-grandson of the Onslow Company leader, Robert Archibald.

So the principals of the Oak Island Association, and their connection to New England, is already known, including that of the Delano and Lynds families.

John Gammell, another Truro Company shareholder, was the son of Robert Gammell. His grandfather, Andrew Gammell, is said to have been born in 1732 in Massachusetts. Andrew married Jane McLellan, who was born in Plymouth, Massachusetts. Their son was Robert Gammell, born in 1765, probably in Nova Scotia.

Note: In Renwick Chappell's booklet, *Read, Think and Reason*, he mistakenly names Gammell as Cammell, or this happened in the transcription of his writings.

Robert Creelman is listed as the Truro Company manager, and was very involved in the search for treasure on Oak Island, on and off, throughout much of his adult life. He was part of the Truro Company from 1849 to 1850, the Oak Island Association from 1863 to 1865, and the Oak Island Treasure Company from 1893 to 1997.

Robert was actually the great-grandson of Colonel Robert Archibald, who is said in most early accounts of the Oak Island story to have been the head of the 1804/05 Onslow Company, the first coordinated group to dig on the island. Robert Archibald was also the brother-in-law of Simeon Lynds of the Onslow Company.

In 1756, three Creelman brothers, Samuel, Matthew and Francis, made the move from Coleraine, County Londonderry, Ireland, to Nova Scotia. Samuel settled in Upper Stewiacke, and the other two elsewhere.

Robert descended from Samuel. However, he had his own New England roots through his family relationship to the Archibald and Lynds families, and likely other Nova Scotian families as well.

There were so many intermarriages, and it's possible that all these early landowners and searchers had some roots in New England on the paternal side, the maternal side, or both.

I could find no lineage for Jotham McCully who acted as manager for the Truro Company.

Another man not mentioned yet was William Gormley, and investor in the Truro Group. McCully records William Gormley as a "financier." The Gormleys were from Pawtucket, Rhode Island, located just 50 miles from Plymouth, and are still numerous there today.

Many dissenting families from the Plymouth Colony moved away to avoid the stricter Puritan rule of early Plymouth and Boston and formed Rhode Island. It may be the Gormley family was one of these. They also have links to New Brunswick and the Annapolis Valley.

According to Scott Clarke:

*The last treasure hunting company to dig on Oak Island during the 19th century was the Oak Island Treasure Company whose membership included Adams A. Tupper, Adams's nephew H.C. (Henry Charles) Tupper, Robert Creelman and Robert's son William Creelman. William would become the fifth generation of Oak Island treasure hunters from that same Archibald-Creelman family!*

*Another young man who joined the Oak Island Treasure Company around 1893 (who was shown briefly on the "Family Album" episode of Curse of Oak Island) was named Frederick Leander Blair.*

*What the show didn't mention is that Fred was a nephew of Isaac Blair and Great Grandson of Onslow Company member William Blair Jr.*

*Frederick Blair would go on to spend the next 60 years of his life involved in excavations on Oak Island.*

Since most of these families have already been well-covered, it seems that we can safely say that the first four organized digs, all during the 19th century, had more than their fair share of New Englanders, some directly from Plymouth, some from nearby Boston, and some from other parts of New England.

One company that did no actual work on the island, but leased it in 1865 for a treasure search, was the Oak Island Contract Company. Oak Island was leased by Anthony Graves. Henry George Hill was president and Augustus Oliver (A.O.) Creighton was the treasurer.

Creighton fits into the story in other ways, as well, especially concerning the so-called 90 foot stone, which was said to be found at about the 90 foot level in the Money Pit, and which had strange inscriptions on it that were never satisfactorily deciphered.

The Creightons have roots in both Nova Scotia and New Hampshire, and this I know for certain because of my own family's relationship to the Creighton family.

Other men involved on Oak Island along the way were named MacDonald, Hill, Fraser, Mitchell and the like, probably names too common to be accurately traced.

In the case of MacDonald, at least we know William Alexander's full name ended with MacDonald and the current premier Knight Baronet of Nova Scotia is Sir Ian MacDonald MacUisdean.

The article that brought so many treasure seekers to Oak Island was written by David MacDonald, who passed away just a couple of years ago. David wrote an article called "The Mystery of Oak Island," which was published in *Reader's Digest*, in January of 1965, and which inspired many people to come to the island.

Other than the Roosevelt/Bowdoin/Childs attempt at treasure recovery on Oak Island in 1909, most of the 20th century (and beyond) treasure hunts were carried out by people from all over the United States and Canada, and have no real purpose in our discussion. But there can be no doubt that in the early years of land ownership and treasure hunting on Oak Island there was a definite connection to the *Mayflower*, the **Mayflower Compact**, and New England in general.

In 2018, while on my second visit to Oak Island, Rick Lagina told me that he needed a quote from me. At first I wasn't sure what he meant.

It was made clear to me that he would like some special words of mine to be placed on the wall of the Oak Island Interpretive Centre alongside quotes from other significant authors and searchers on Oak Island.

Of course, I was highly honored at this request. But I wanted to take my time and think it over.

When I returned home I sat quietly in my office thinking about what I should say.

I knew that the search on Oak Island wasn't about one special person, one theory, or one attempt at recovery.

It was much bigger than that.

It seemed to me that the search was about hope – hope for something that would allow a person to escape the troubles of this world, laced with hope that something fantastic could be dug from the ground after a burial of many centuries that might prove invaluable.

And then I realized what it was I needed to say. Here is my quote that graces the Interpretive Centre wall just above the *Reader's Digest* article.

*"Oak Island is not so much a mystery to be solved as it is a chance to experience the unapologetic fascination of youth once again."*

"Oak Island is not so much a mystery to be solved, as it is a chance to experience the unapologetic fascinatio of youth once again."

James A. McQuiston - Author

"I think I was never governed by lust of treasure recovery myse I was more interested in a solution of the mystery."

Gilbert Hedden letter to R.V. Harris in 1953

*This photo from my time on Oak Island shows me standing below my quote, which appears on an Oak Island Interpretive Centre wall. Directly behind me is a display of the original **Reader's Digest** article that was responsible for so many of us becoming interested in the Oak Island mystery.*

*Chapter Nine*

## SUPPORT FOR MY THEORY

As I walked alongside Rick Lagina to return to the Oak Island Interpretive Centre, after a very long war room meeting, he said something to the effect that "Yours was one of the best presentations we've ever had."

He explained, "We get a lot of theorists in the war room that come here to tell us their theory but then have no evidence to back it up. We sit there wondering what questions to even ask them. You came with all the questions already answered."

Beyond being happy that this was the case, I was also pleased that all my hard work, all the endless hours of reading old documents, and sometimes staying up nearly all night long putting the Oak Island puzzle together, was finally being recognized by someone who mattered.

Others, like co-investor Craig Tester, island historian Charles Barkhouse, and especially Nova Scotia historian Doug Crowell (all intimately involved in the Oak Island search) have been very helpful in providing answers, directing me to new sources of information, and steering me on the correct course. There were many others who corresponded with me about Oak Island, and some who wrote about Oak Island in ways that support my theory, before I even started my research or writing my books.

*This is my favorite photo of Rick Lagina and I (standing outside a sandwich shop near New Ross).*

In fact, it was the Oak Island team that urged me to write my first two books, *Oak Island Missing Links* and *Oak Island 1632*.

This was because I had traded so much information with them mostly existing only in our emails and in my first war room presentation in 2017.

By the way, I was the very last person to present in the old war room. They immediately moved to a duplicate building, a much sturdier one, with better climate control, and located well beyond the reach of the typical tourists visiting the island while filming was taking place.

I would go on to participate in five war room meetings, and I knew I had to write the follow up books, *Oak Island Knights* and *Oak Island Endgame*, in order to tell the complete tale.

With each book I was sure I was finished writing about Oak Island.

One day, I commented to my son that I wished that all of my books could be put together as one, but that's just not how this whole thing developed. That's when he suggested I write a historical fiction version of my theory, which I did, and called it *Oak Island The Novel*.

During the writing of *Oak Island Endgame* I began to become aware of the many connections to the Plymouth Colony and, after sending several emails on this subject to the Oak Island team, I thought I better write at least one more book just to get this research recorded.

The fact that the Oak Island team has stayed interested in this research for so long is one of the best endorsements I could get for my theory.

Earlier in this book I spoke of at least five authors who also mentioned Sir William Alexander as perhaps playing a role in the Oak Island mystery.

These authors would be:

- Reginald Harris, *The Oak Island Mystery*, 1967
- Mark Finnan, *The First Nova Scotian*, 1977
- Joan Harris (Hope), *A Castle in Nova Scotia*, 1997
- Michael Bradley, *Grail Knights of North America*, 1998
- Cort Lindhal, *Oak Island & Arcadian Mysteries*, 2018

I am not making the claim that any one of the people I have mentioned have whole-heatedly endorsed my theory. What I am saying, however, is that many have previously written about William Alexander's possible connection to the Oak Island mystery.

Others have verified certain parts of my research.

Overall, a great many authors through the ages have lent support to my theory in their recording of aged documents, land deeds, knighthood charters, and even books.

What I am speaking of here are modern authors who have helped me come up with my theory, in most cases unknowingly, and who published their books before mine, or at least published their basic ideas.

Some more recent Oak Island authors like Randall Sullivan and D'Arcy O'Connor do not even mention William Alexander, and Sullivan leaves out of his Oak Island time line any mention of 1621 as the year Nova Scotia was founded and named, or William Alexander as the proprietor of this land from 1621 through 1632.

I do not mention this as a criticism of these authors, but rather to show just how complex and varied the study of Oak Island can be.

Each researcher seems to come at this from his or her own point of view and special interests. Since I have been focused on Scottish history for decades, this has been my point of view.

One thing that Sullivan did write, which supports my theory, is the part about how, if the three original discoverers of the Money Pit did in fact find rotting, moss covered tree stumps and some new growth of trees, this would mean the original burial of whatever was in the Money Pit could have only taken place in the 17th century. He states further that the Oak Island team has enlisted the help of some tree experts who seem to verify this belief. Of course, my date of 1632 is smack dab in the 17th century.

Often recognized as the first person to write a book about Oak Island, Reginald Harris, Past Grand Master of Freemasonry, was also first to imply that William Alexander could have something to do with Oak Island, in his book *The Oak Island Mystery*. His mention of Alexander was brief, but nevertheless, he made that mention. Ultimately, I was aided by three people with the surname of Harris.

Graham Harris and Les MacPhie wrote the book *Oak Island And It's Lost Treasure*, in which they state: "We estimate that digging from shaft to bedrock would have taken a crew of sturdy men (probably seafarers) no longer than three to four months to complete."

This comports with my theory of a two to three month creation of the Money Pit (happening sometime between April and June, 1632, in my version of the story).

This was echoed in letters written by Oak Island landowner/searcher Gilbert Hedden, who not only agreed with the assessment of the amount of time it would have taken, but also mentioned 1630 and 1635 as potential dates for the creation of the Money Pit.

Graham Harris had passed away by the time I was able to reach out about his and MacPhie's book.

However, Les MacPhie was very amendable to trading our respective books and ideas. After reading one of my books, he wrote to say: "Congratulations. I find that the book is well-researched and that the theory is credible."

The third Harris to indirectly support my theory was Joan Harris, who went by the pen name Joan Hope. She too has passed away.

In her book *A Castle In Nova Scotia*, she was first to bring notice to the mysterious foundation located at New Ross, just twenty or so miles up Gold River from Oak Island, where the 1671 knighthood medallion was found. One of Joan's theories implied that the Alexander family may have been responsible for building it. She asked the question: "What if the Oak Island pit had also been used by emissaries of Charles I?"

These emissaries would have been William Alexander and his Knights Baronet of Nova Scotia. She even points out that one Thomas Hope, presumably some type of ancestor of Joan, was made a Knight Baronet of Nova Scotia in 1629.

She cites the charter of 1621 given to Sir William Alexander, which read, in part:

*It hath seemed meet to us, and we will that it shall be lawful to the said Sir William, and his aforesaid, to build, or to cause to be built, one or more strong holds, fortresses, castles, forts, towers, depots of arms, blockhouses, and other edifices.*

This portion of the charter specifically allowed Sir William Alexander to build dwellings such as the one whose foundation can be just barely seen at New Ross.

Michael Bradley, author of *Grail Knights of North America*, echoed Joan Harris's suggestion that the site was later occupied by Scottish royalty during the time of Cromwell.

Bradley writes that the Nauss family of Lunenburg claim they were brought to the area in 1623 to construct a mansion and that an anonymous Nauss descendant produced sketches of the building based on family lore.

He goes on to repeat Joan's belief, suggesting that the structure was "purposely and efficiently" destroyed at some unspecified later date possibly by Cromwell's forces in 1654-56.

We know that Cromwell's man Sedgwick was in Nova Scotia in 1654 to force submission of anyone who would threaten Cromwell's rule. This theory supports my contention that the ruins don't appear to have crumbled through the normal wear and tear of time.

It should be stated that this area was not called New Ross during the time of the Alexander presence.

I was extremely lucky to have corresponded with the Nauss descendant mentioned – one John Nauss.

Again, I am not saying that Mr. Nauss is endorsing my theory, I am only relaying a few of the comments he made, which do seem to support my work. These are excerpts from a number of emails we shared:

• "Jim, Enjoying the read so far. Wish I could drop everything and read all at once."

• "I am the John Nauss to whom the book is dedicated for many reasons, notably I was there every step of the way."

• "I am the remaining living person involved in the whole affair."

• "As for what is written in Joan's book, those are stories I was told by my grandfather who chose me to hold the family 'secrets' and, over a period of two to three years, he let me know them. Like all family legends, that is what they were, some embellishments and some just stories, but a lot could be based on 'truth', whatever that is."

• "Joan sometimes referred to my stories as the 'Nauss Documents' or the like, for brevity sake. It was mostly based on oral tradition."

Another man I was very pleased to correspond with was Mark Finnan, a wonderful Nova Scotia historian.

In his great book *The First Nova Scotian*, Finnan speaks briefly of the Baronets of Nova Scotia, and his very last sentence in that book reads, in part, "...perhaps the full story of the earliest known Scottish link to Nova Scotia has yet to be told."

Also, from *The First Nova Scotian*, while commenting on his earlier book *Oak Island Secrets*, Finnan states:

> *In my two years of research for* **Oak Island Secrets** *I became increasingly aware that Sir William Alexander might have been associated with, or aware of the work which, according to the radio carbon dating of organic materials found on the island, went on there sometime in the 16th to 17th century.*
>
> *In the absence of any documentation or other supporting historical evidence, one can only theorize that Alexander knew of a plan to hide and preserve something of great value on Oak Island... his extensive philosophical interest, his commercial mining activities, his powerful connections at court, and his association with men involved in the then-emerging Masonic movement in Scotland and England all point strongly to that possibility.*

At this point, I was liking what I was reading in his Oak Island/Nova Scotia books, and deeply appreciated his openness and our conversations.

Another man who has written extensively on Oak Island, and was part of the #1 theory out of 25, is Cort Lindhal. Although we don't agree 100% on the set of circumstances surrounding the Money Pit, Cort has many times referred to Sir William Alexander as being at least marginally involved, if not to a greater extent.

Out of the handful of emails we exchanged, this comment stands out: "James, that is basically what I found as well, with a few minor differences."

Sometimes it feels a little lonely being the only person consistently preaching the Alexander/Knights Baronet theory for the solution to the Oak Island mystery.

I have been simply overwhelmed with all the details that have been found and I always fear I will overwhelm the reader as well.

The proof, at least for me, seems to be in the historical documentation. And being a very pragmatic person, this suits me just fine. I don't need stars in the sky, or mythological solutions. – "Just the facts Ma'am" as the old TV saying goes.

We have the actual wording from William Alexander's grant for Nova Scotia. We have the actual words of Sir Ferdinando Gorges, Sir William Alexander, King James I and King Charles I, all concerning the fact that Nova Scotia was granted to Alexander as a way to disperse the French that were living there in order to protect the *Mayflower* Pilgrims.

We have the actual wording of the charter for the Knights Baronet of Nova Scotia, of the original charter for Mirligaiche from William Alexander to Claude de la Tour, and the words of the charter for Mirligaiche from Charles de la Tour to Thomas Temple.

We have the genealogies of dozens, if not hundreds, of people recorded and reported by members of those families, and collected through my research, showing a potential link of anywhere from six to ten men important to Oak Island history who were connected to signers of the **Mayflower Compact**, and more who came out of Plymouth or nearby areas.

We have the Freemason minutes from 1634 showing how the first recorded, non-operative, accepted Masons were connected to the Knights Baronet of Nova Scotia.

We have the Freemason records commenting on the robbery carried out by Alexander Strachan, along with the Privy Council minutes, and the court records detailing not only the case against Strachan, but also the actual contents of the stolen items.

We have the words of Captain Robert MacKinnon describing, in his book *Shipwrecked North of 40*, how he found a ship dated to around 1600 within sight of Oak Island, and how it contained silverware with a stag emblem on the handles, the stag being the symbol of Clan Strachan since at least 1309.

We have weather reports from NOAA showing the Port Royal side of Nova Scotia generally having milder weather in early spring than the Atlantic side. We have their reports for the last few years showing gale force winds of 25-40 knots and waves from 20 to 40 feet, plus fog and freezing spray, as projected weather conditions for the North Atlantic in April.

We have much older reports from Jacques Cartier and Samuel de Champlain indicating very rough, cold weather in early spring around Nova Scotia, as outlined in my *Oak Island Endgame* book.

Jacques Cartier wrote that, from mid-November 1535 to mid-April 1536, his French fleet lay frozen solid at the mouth of the St. Charles River near Quebec. Ice was over a fathom (1.8m or about 6 feet) thick on the river, with snow piled four feet (1.2m) deep ashore.

Cartier's first voyage to North America didn't start until April 20th. His second voyage started on May 19th. His third voyage began on May 23rd – each voyage beginning later in the spring. All of these dates are later than the date by which the Scots were forced to sail, exceeding it by about a month.

We have the words of the order for the Scots to leave Port Royal and head to England, dated March 29, 1632, something that would have been impossible to do.

Then there are the artifacts:

• Wood chips reported by Dave Tobias, Oak Island treasure hunter and landowner, to be from 193 feet deep in the Money Pit area, dated in a range of 1490 to 1660;

• A log window sill dated in a range of 1530 to 1760;

• An oak peg dated to 1517 to 1835;

• A piece of axe cut wood was found at depth near the Money Pit, dated to as old as 1626;

• Another significant piece of wood, found *in situ* in the eye of the swamp, dated to as early as 1619.

Dr. Ian Spooner, a wetlands expert, has stated that there is evidence of substantial man-made constructs in the swamp dating to the early 1600s.

Other carbon dating records belonging to the current Oak Island team, and to the two longtime Oak Island landowner/searchers, Fred Nolan and Dan Blankenship, show dates that could also fit my 1632 date.

Also, there were shoes found in the mud off a sunken wharf that were dated to before 1700, based on their construction; the same for some forged nails found around the island, based on their carbon content.

The ship planking found in the swamp dated into the 1600s, as did the scissors from Smith's Cove. Plus the piece of red jewelry found by metal detectorist Gary Drayton was dated as 400 to 500 years old; and even human bones which were dated as early as the 1600s.

Carbon dating and artifact dating are not always exact sciences, but with so many pointing to the 17th century, this has to be taken seriously as the time period for the creation of the Money Pit.

The list is long – historical time lines, artifact dating, written documents, family genealogies, a missing stolen treasure, the work of other researchers, and my nearly five years of almost constant investigation. These have led me to believe that I have the answer, or very close to the answer, as to what precipitated the Oak Island mystery. But, based on past experience, I suspect I will not give up on my research, and I and others, as well, will contribute new and exciting finds as the years, and the "unapologetic fascination," continue on.

# Acknowledgments

This is my sixth book on Oak Island. With every book my wife, Elizabeth McQuiston, has patiently dealt with my spending endless hours researching and writing, and she has just as patiently proofread the author's copies, correcting my errors and making helpful suggestions.

I especially wish to thank her for making my books better than they would otherwise be.

The last few books have also been proofread by my cousin, Patricia Gustafson, who has spent many years teaching the art of writing to her students. She, too, has caught my errors, and has made many helpful edits.

Beyond this, I would like to thank the members of the Oak Island crew who have helped and believed in my work – Rick and Marty Lagina, Craig Tester, Doug Crowell, Charles Barkhouse and the rest. This would extend to the many unnamed Prometheus Entertainment producers and staff who have facilitated my travels to Oak Island, and my appearances in the war room.

Finally, to all the other authors, clerks, and family historians, ancient and modern, whose work I have built upon, I am very grateful for the hours you have spent recording individual threads of history that have allowed me to create this larger tapestry of human endeavor.

# Epilogue

If I said this would be my last book on the subject of Oak Island, I could possibly be fooling myself. But I have no idea what more there is to even write about.

I've stayed away from discussing the goings on during the actual searches for treasure, simply because this has been covered by so many people. Also, this happened after the fact – after the treasure had already been buried for many years.

Of all the items pulled from the Money Pit, the most significant for me is the piece of parchment. The very last item on the list of treasure stolen by Alexander Strachan was a waxed canvas bag filled with parchment deeds for castles owned by the man he had robbed.

When this piece of parchment was brought up on the end of a drill bit, it had been lying in a flooded pit for several decades, and yet the ink was not smeared, indicating it had been in a waterproof container until that container was punctured by the drill bit. The only waterproof container used back then was a waxed canvas bag, and so the Oak Island parchment fits the description of the last item on the treasure list perfectly.

In recent years, more parchment was brought up from the pit, which was ink-stained from sitting in water.

Little things like this parchment can build and build to show at least what might have happened. That's the way all of my research has been. A thread of history here matches a thread of history there until we see a pattern emerge.

Yes, we may be figuratively looking through the back side of this tapestry, but at least we can get a rough idea of what the design was meant to be.

In my *Oak Island The Novel* book I tried to portray the humanity of the characters in a way that most people could relate to.

Sir William Alexander, the main actor in this tale, was exceptionally well educated and well read. He was given one opportunity after another, and was literally given a land nearly as large as Scotland for his very own. This land was virgin territory with endless forests, fur bearing animals, valuable minerals, clean air and water, plus lots of beautiful shorelines.

Nova Scotia was his paradise and he wished to create from it a utopia where men and women could live freely, escaping the troubles of the old world, from religious wars to plagues, from courtly intrigues to dangerous towns and overland roads.

He offered a knighthood to many men, mostly clan chieftains, who would not otherwise have gained one in their lifetime, and he offered them a share of this land, and a chance to start over in the New World, in a New Scotland, in Nova Scotia.

Due to the duplicity of Charles I, and a constant effort by France to regain their land of Acadia, he failed.

The Alexander family fell apart along with all of their fortune. William died a lonely man, with nearly all of his sons dead, or perhaps escaping to Nova Scotia. He died a poor man, with his creditors arresting his corpse to have it buried on the spot. He died with a fair share of the blame for the British civil war on his shoulders.

Sir William Alexander, a man who dealt with two kings, with Sir Francis Bacon, and Sir Ferdinando Gorges (in the earliest settlement in America), who once stated that he never remembered anything as fondly as America, a man who facilitated the initiation of his sons and friends as the world's first recorded non-operative Masons (or what we now know as Freemasons) – this man nearly faded into obscurity!

And yet his positive accomplishments included helping with the very settling of America, with creating and naming the land called Nova Scotia, and with creating a knighthood, still in existence today – all of this happening 400 years ago.

Talk about having a long-lasting effect on history!

I believe the Oak Island mystery began around 400 years ago, as well (1632 to be exact). I may be wrong, or I may be only slightly wrong on some of the details, but all of what I have discovered has to be explained in some way, if not in the way that I have interpreted it.

I've relied almost entirely on documents. When questioned, I produced more documents. Some say history is written by the victors, and while this may be true in the big picture, many day-to-day activities were written down by clerks and by family storytellers.

Within this vast myriad of seemingly unconnected notations, with no particularly ulterior motive or hidden agenda driving them, is where I have found the bulk of the threads for the tapestry I have woven.

In the grand scheme of life, my writings may not mean that much but, in the history of the Oak Island mystery I believe they are substantial and I think that this belief is held by other critical players as well.

Everyone loves a mystery that is just about ready to be solved. It is one of the most addictive pastimes a person can engage in.

It is estimated that *The Curse of Oak Island* TV show has about ten million fans around the world, and it is often the number one cable TV show on the air during its season. I've appeared on this show many times by now, and my theory is currently rated as #6 out of 25.

Of course, I think it should be #1 – and it is still a work in progress.

Perhaps the research I've done will be combined with the powerful spell that this show has cast across the world to tell the tale of Sir William Alexander's successes (and failures) as a lesson in dreaming big, but carefully.

Perhaps my story will entertain or, even better, lead others to more significant discoveries.

I've enjoyed it. I probably will continue to enjoy it. And I am thankful for all who have supported this effort to uncover the true story of the Oak Island mystery.

Until next time, stay safe, and enjoy any chance you get to experience your own unapologetic fascination.

## More Books By This Author

I have published several non-fiction books on Oak Island, and on lesser-known historical figures, plus two historical fiction works in the same vein, all based around hidden or long-forgotten history. All of these books are available on Amazon.

They include:

*Oak Island The Novel* – This book is my attempt to tell the bigger story behind my Oak Island theory, while couching it in the form of a historical fiction novel, full of great love affairs, swashbuckling action, and a stolen treasure. All of the characters are real historic figures and all of the major events are real, as well.

*Oak Island Endgame* – My first three non-fiction Oak Island books focused on the events leading up to the burial of treasure on Oak Island. With this book, I began looking at the people who came to Oak Island as soon as it was safe to go there, either to settle as landowners or to search for treasure. This book led, eventually, to the book you are reading, *Oak Island And The Mayflower*.

*Oak Island Knights* – I reveal a massive treasure stolen in Scotland that appears to have been at least partially intended to finance Nova Scotia and that, due to unexpected circumstances, may have ended up buried on Oak Island. I also explore a 1671 knighthood medallion that was found at New Ross up Gold River about twenty miles from Oak Island.

*Oak Island 1632* – My second book on Oak Island pinpoints a specific year for the beginning of the Oak Island mystery. In it is revealed, for the first time ever, that the world's first recorded non-operative Masons all had connections to the Scots adventure in Nova Scotia, dating from 1621 to 1656. I tell how these Scots were forced to leave in bad weather, which caused them to take shelter on Oak Island.

*Oak Island Missing Links* – This was my first Oak Island book. I take a look at the various legends surrounding Oak Island, NS, with some very plausible interpretations of the legends of Glooscap and Henry Sinclair. I also discuss the Knights Templar at length.

*Captain Jack: Father of the Yukon* – The story of the first 25 years before the Klondike Gold Rush, and the man who led the way, earning, in his own lifetime, the monikers of "Father of the Yukon," "Father of Alaska," "Injun Papa," and "Yukon Jack."

*Ebenezer Denny: First Mayor of Pittsburgh* – This is the story of a man who had already led a full life as a privateer and a Revolutionary War hero, and who wrote the most-often quoted description of the surrender of the British at Yorktown, before becoming the first mayor of this important frontier town.

*Patrick's Run* – This is a historical fiction account of Patrick Fitzpatrick, a hero of the War of 1812, who was executed for a crime he didn't commit, causing Michigan to become the first English-speaking territory in history to outlaw the death penalty.

## REFERENCE MATERIAL

I've used many resources over the years to understand Scottish history. A few worth mentioning, in regard to my Knights Baronet of Nova Scotia research, are listed here in chronological order, by year of publication.

Without a doubt, the most valuable were *The Registry of the Privy Council of Scotland, An Encouragement To Colonies, History of the Lodge of Edinburgh #1, Memorials of the Earl of Stirling And The House of Alexander,* plus *Memorials of the Scottish Families of Strachan and Wise,* each of which provided invaluable information.

•*The Registry of the Privy Council of Scotland* – those volumes regarding the Baronets of Nova Scotia, and spanning the mid-16th through the mid-17th centuries

•*Works of Samuel de Champlain,* Samuel de Champlain, 1610-18

•*An Encouragement To Colonies,* Sir William Alexander, 1624

•*The Peerage of Scotland,* Sir Robert Douglas, 1764

•*Records of the Colony of New Plymouth, in New England,* by Nathaniel Bradstreet, 1810-1874, ed; David Pulsifer, 1802-1894, ed

•*Royal Letters, Charters, and Tracts Relating to the Colonization of New Scotland and the Institution of the Order of The Knights Baronet of Nova Scotia 1621 – 1638,* The Bannatyne Club, 1827

•*Sketch of the History of the Knights Templar,* James Burnes, 1840

•*A History of Nova-Scotia, or Acadie,* James Barnes, 1865

•*The History of Scotland,* John Hill Burton, 1870

•*Documentary History of the State of Maine,* Maine Historial Society, *1869-1916*

•*The Old Charges of Freemasons,* William Hughan, 1872

• *History of the Lodge of Edinburgh #1,* David Lyon, 1873

•*Memorials of the Earl of Stirling and of the House of Alexander,* Rev. Charles Rogers, 1877

•*Memorials of the Scottish Families of Strachan and Wise,* Rev. Charles Rogers, 1877

•*The Scottish Master Mason's Handbook,* Frederick Crowe, 1894

•*The Freemason's Repository,* Several Authors, 1897

•*Annals of the North British Society, Halifax, Nova Scotia, 1768-1903,* James S. MacDonald, 1903

•*Complete Baronetage,* George Cokayne, 1904

•*Proceedings of the Society of Antiquaries of Scotland, 1925-1926,* D. Hay Fleming (article), 1926

•*Sir William Alexander, First Earl of Stirling,* Thomas McGrail, 1940

•*The Surnames of Scotland,* George Black, 1946

•*Clan Donald,* Donald MacDonald, 1978

• *Secret Treasure of Oak Island*, D'Arcy O'Connor, 1978

• *The Origins of Freemasonry*, David Stevenson, 1988

• *The First Nova Scotian*, Mark Finnan, 1997

• *Oak Island Secrets*, Mark Finnan, 1997

• *Grail Knights of North America*, Michael Bradley, 1998

• *Nation and Province in the First British Empire*, edited by Ned Landsman, 2001

• *Freemasonry on Both Sides of the Atlantic*, Richard Weisberger, Wallace McLeod, and S. Brent Morris, 2002

• *Oak Island and Its Lost Treasure*, Graham Harris and Les MacPhie, 2005, revised 2013

• *Terror of The Seas: Scottish Maritime Warfare 1513-1713*, Steve Murdoch, 2010

• *The Curse of Oak Island*, Randall Sullivan, 2018

• *Shipwrecked North of 40*, Robert MacKinnon, 2018

• *The Oak Island Encyclopedia*, Hammerson Peters, 2019

Websites accessed in September 2020:

www.monstersandcritics.com/author/scott-clarke/

www.oakislandcompendium.ca

www.plimoth.org

www.themayflowersociety.org

www.massmayflower.org/index.php/20-research/117-plymouth-colony-resources

THE END
(at least for now)

Printed in Great Britain
by Amazon

23714295R00096